Resurrecting Old-Fashioned
Foundationalism

Studies in Epistemology and Cognitive Theory
Series Editor: *Paul K. Moser, Loyola University of Chicago*

Resurrecting Old-Fashioned Foundationalism

EDITED BY
MICHAEL R. DEPAUL

ROWMAN & LITTLEFIELD PUBLISHERS, INC.
Lanham • Boulder • New York • Oxford

ROWMAN & LITTLEFIELD PUBLISHERS, INC.

Published in the United States of America
by Rowman & Littlefield Publishers, Inc.
4720 Boston Way, Lanham, Maryland 20706
http://www.rowmanlittlefield.com

12 Hid's Copse Road
Cumnor Hill, Oxford OX2 9JJ, England

British Library Cataloguing in Publication Information Available

Library of Congress Cataloging-in-Publication Data

Resurrecting old-fashioned foundationalism / edited by Michael R. DePaul.
    p. cm. – (Studies in epistemology and cognitive theory)
    Includes bibliographical references and index.
    ISBN 0-8476-9288-4 (alk. paper) – ISBN 0-8476-9289-2 (pbk. : alk. paper)
    1. Knowledge, Theory of. I. DePaul, Michael R. (Michael Raymond), 1954- II.
Studies in epistemology and cognitive theory (Unnumbered)

    BD161 .R483 2001
    121—dc21

                                                                00-059059

Printed in the United States of America
⊖™ The paper used in this publication meets the minimum requirements of American
National Standard for Information Sciences—Permanence of Paper for Printed Library
Materials, ANSI/NISO Z39.48–1992.

Contents

Preface

Epistemic foundationalism has been subjected to various and furious assaults. It is easy to find authors discussing the implications of foundationalism's collapse. So one who has a passing familiarity with the recent literature in philosophy and related disciplines might easily get the impression that foundationalism is dead. But foundationalism is alive and well; indeed, at least within Anglo-American analytic philosophy, I think it is safe to say that it remains the dominant position. One might begin to get a more accurate impression if one thinks about the din of the attacks on foundationalism after noting that there are not a lot of protests against a country like Iceland—one does not hear people calling Iceland the Great Satan nor does one see the Icelandic flag being burned by angry mobs. In this respect the scholarly world is much like the world of politics: a good way to find out which positions are powerful is to see which ones are being attacked most harshly. To be perfectly fair, however, I must point out that the situation is somewhat more complicated. More careful examination of the literature reveals that the kind of foundationalism now widely accepted is rather different from the old-fashioned sort of foundationalism that those who have pronounced foundationalism dead probably had in mind. Given that virtually all the friends of foundationalism have moved on to accept more newfangled versions, one might conclude that insofar as the critics had the old-fashioned form in mind, they were right about foundationalism's doom. But things change. As the saying goes, "Everything old is new again." The contributions to this volume by Richard Fumerton and Laurence BonJour make an important effort to resurrect a rather old-fashioned form of foundationalism. But I am getting ahead of myself. I need to explain the difference between what I am thinking of as old-fashioned foundationalism and the currently more popular newfangled variety.

The place to begin any discussion of foundationalism is with the regress argument.[1] According to this ancient argument, when we consider a belief that is justified[2] and ask how it is that the belief is justified, we are typically led to another belief that supports the first. When we ask about the second belief, we may well be led to a third. The third may in turn lead to a fourth, and so on. But how long can things go on in this fashion? There would seem to be only three possibilities: the chain of beliefs either goes on forever, circles back upon itself, or stops. Finding the first two possibilities unacceptable, foundationalists opt for the third, holding that there are some beliefs that are justified, but that are not justified by any further beliefs. The regress stops with such basic or foundational beliefs, and any other beliefs that are justified must be supported by the foundational basic beliefs.

So, foundationalists typically accept two doctrines:

The Foundations Doctrine:
If any beliefs are justified, then some of the justified beliefs (i.e., the foundational beliefs) are not justified in virtue of their logical or evidential relations to other beliefs.

The Superstructure Doctrine:
Any justified nonfoundational belief is justified, at least in part,[3] in virtue of its logical or evidential relations to foundational beliefs.

These two doctrines obviously leave many questions unanswered. One wants to know which beliefs are foundational and one wants an account of how it is that these beliefs are justified—in virtue of what do they have their special status? One wants to know which logical and evidential relations allow one belief to support another. More specifically, once the foundational beliefs are identified, one will want to have an account of how various sorts of beliefs we ordinarily take ourselves to be justified in holding are justified by these basic beliefs. The various versions of foundationalism differ in terms of the answers they give to these questions, that is to say, in terms of how they elaborate the foundations and superstructure doctrines.

Let's consider a familiar example. The usual take on Descartes' old-fashioned version of foundationalism construes it as a very austere, rigorous position. Since he was concerned to answer skeptical questions, Descartes required that our foundations be certain. One must be able to see for one's self that one could not be mistaken about a belief for it to be foundational. The only way Descartes was willing to build upon these very secure foundations was via deduction. And not just any deduction: in order to add a belief one must see that it is a deductive consequence of the foundations, one must clearly perceive that the foundations guarantee the truth of the belief. The obvious problem with this sort of rigorous foundationalism is that it must regard only a very small portion of our beliefs as justified. Perhaps a person cannot be mistaken about simple logical and mathematical propositions, some simple conceptual truths, mereological principles, and the like. And maybe there are some propositions about one's own mind about which one cannot be mistaken, for example, propositions regarding the nature of one's current sensory experience or what one believes or desires. But even being very generous about what will count as a certain foundation, we will have very little to go on, and with deduction as our only mortar, we just are not going to be able to build very high.

Foundationalists after Descartes have learned the lesson of his failure well. There certainly are not many advocates of infallibilism around these days. And a surprising number of epistemologists are not even particularly interested in addressing the kinds of skeptical concerns with which Descartes began. The following line of thought has come to be widely accepted, influencing both the way in which epistemologists conceive of their project and the substantive positions they adopt:

In order to answer epistemological questions, we need to have a clear understanding of what justification is. But we cannot just say, off the tops of our heads, what justification involves. This is something that we must work out. And when we try to work it out, we have no choice but to rely upon the intuitively clear cases of justified and unjustified beliefs. It is these paradigm cases that provide the best evidence regarding the content of our epistemic concepts. What we must do, therefore, is work out an account or, if we are lucky, a full-blown analysis of justification that manages to classify all the clear cases the right way.

Widespread adoption of this methodological position obviously has not led to unanimity on all counts. But when we view epistemological questions from this perspective it becomes quite clear that Descartes simply set the standards far too high. Considered on their own, various propositions that are crucial to the Cartesian outlook may seem compelling, for example, that a person cannot be justified in believing something if he or she might be mistaken about it or that one belief could only be justified on the basis of another if the believer can see that the truth of the second guarantees the truth of the first. But when we test these sorts of propositions against the clear cases, they just do not hold up.

Let's take as an example an ordinary perceptual belief: My wife is reading in the living room on a sunny afternoon, hears a noise at the window, looks up from her book, and sees the familiar form of her beloved cat "Boogins" scratching at the window to be let in. She forms the belief that Boogins is at the window. Such a belief would seem to constitute an obvious example of a justified belief even though it is quite clear that the belief does not satisfy Cartesian standards. What, then, explains how the belief is justified? More old-fashioned forms of foundationalism that stick closer to the Cartesian model would seek to begin by formulating a proposition that captures what is given to the believer by sensation. Typically this will be a belief regarding the character of her perceptual experience, e.g., "It seems to me that I am seeing Boogins scratching at the window in his usual insistent way." Such a belief seems on its face like a good bet for stopping a regress of justification. The person who has the perceptual experience can just tell that the belief regarding the character of this experience is true. Perhaps such a belief is not certain or infallible, but it approaches being so. A belief about the character of one's current perceptual experience seems to provide a great example of a foundational belief: it is sufficiently secure from error that its claim to be justified is very plausible, yet it seems clear that such a belief is not supported by other beliefs. The next step for the old-fashioned foundationalist would be to construct an argument to support a belief about actual objects, in the present example, the belief that Boogins the cat is scratching at the window, on the basis of the belief regarding the nature of the believer's visual experience.

Newfangled forms of foundationalism typically begin diverging from the more old-fashioned versions with the observation that in ordinary cases we almost never form beliefs regarding the nature of our perceptual experiences. We simply have the experiences and form beliefs about the world around us. In an ordinary case like the example involving my wife and Boogins, where she is looking at a nearby, familiar object in broad daylight, where her vision is normal, she is not under the influence of any drugs, has no reason to doubt herself, etc., we would regard her belief that Boogins is at the window as justified. Indeed, this belief would seem to be a paradigm case of a justified belief. Various forms of newfangled foundationalism have different stories to tell about how my wife's belief comes to have the status of being justified. Some might point to the reliability of such beliefs, others to the fact that the belief is produced by a properly functioning cognitive mechanism. Some might simply point to the belief's having been formed as a result of a certain particular sensory experience. But the various accounts will tend to agree in taking the plot of the epistemological story to parallel the story about the formation of the belief. Most significantly, since my wife did not form her belief regarding Boogins by inferring it from any other belief, and she does not have any beliefs at all about the nature of her visual experience that could stand in logical or evidential relation to her belief about Boogins, they will be willing to take her belief that Boogins is at the window as justified on its own. Thus, these versions of foundationalism are willing to take this and similar beliefs about ordinary objects as foundational.

Both the old-fashioned and newfangled forms of foundationalism regard perceptual beliefs as justified. But the newfangled version cleaves more closely to the methodological position I articulated above. The newfangled foundationalism can accept that ordinary perceptual beliefs, as they are ordinarily formed, are justified. Ordinarily these beliefs are automatically formed upon the having of certain sensory experiences. The are not typically inferred from beliefs about the nature of these sensory experiences. Indeed, people usually do not form any beliefs about the nature of their perceptual experiences, so they generally will not even have the sorts of foundational beliefs singled out by the old-fashioned foundationalists as basic around to serve as the premises for inferences to beliefs about the "external world." Hence, it would be more accurate to say that newfangled foundationalists can accept ordinary perceptual beliefs as actually justified, while old-fashioned foundationalists can say only that such beliefs can become justified—if the believer forms an appropriate belief about the nature of her sensory experience and makes appropriate inferential connections between this belief and her belief about the world. For their part, old-fashioned foundationalists will resist the account preferred by the newfangled foundationalsits on the grounds that they hold beliefs to be foundational even though these beliefs do not have a sufficiently strong epistemic status. They will point out that when a person has a certain sensory experience and forms a belief about the nature of that experience, she is in an excellent position to determine that her belief is accurate. While it may not literally be impossible for a person to be mistaken about such a belief, the chance for error is vanishingly small; hence, such beliefs are justified. This aspect of the old-fashioned foundationalists's view constitutes another departure from the methodological position I described above, since the old-fashioned foundationalist seems to be relying upon preconceived notions of what is required for justification rather than allowing this to be determined by analysis based upon what we consider to be paradigm cases of justified belief.

Perhaps old-fashioned foundationalism's lack of psychological realism is sufficient to seal its fate, but it faces another serious problem, a problem that has been seen as particularly damning because it concerns the status of foundational beliefs. One of the defining elements of old-fashioned foundationalism is its acceptance of a serious doctrine of the given. It holds that perceptual knowledge is grounded in sensory experience. The basic beliefs that serve as the foundations for our beliefs about the world are not justified by other beliefs, but they are justified only in virtue of their unique connection with our sensory experience. The point is sometimes put by saying that these beliefs are grounded in, rather than justified by, sensory experience. But there is a well-known objection to this view that is usually put in the form of a dilemma. The sensory experiences that are supposed to ground our foundational beliefs are in some sense propositional or they are not. If they are not propositional in any significant sense, then they cannot be said to require justification, but it is difficult to see how they could stand in the sort of relation to beliefs, which are propositional, which would account for the beliefs being justified. After all, the paradigm cases of such relations are the logical and evidential relations that hold among propositions. If sensory experiences are held to be propositional, or quasi-propositional, then there may not be any difficulty in conceiving of them as relating to beliefs in such a way as to account for the beliefs being justified, but it would seem questions must be raised about the epistemic status of the experiences themselves. Since they are not being conceived of as brute facts, but as having propositional contents, we need to know whether or not they are justified, or quasi-justified, and how it is that they have this status, for if they do not have some such positive epistemic status, it would not seem that any beliefs could be justified in virtue of being grounded in them.

These problems were just too much for the old-fashioned forms of foundationalism and they passed away. Such views could be studied as a chapter in the history of analytic philosophy, but within contemporary epistemology one found only the newfangled form of foundationalism with its common sense methodology, psychological realism, and studied avoidance of any worrisome doctrine of the given. Or so it seemed. In 1997 I began to notice signs of life from old-fashioned foundationalism. I read Richard Fumerton's *Metaepistemology and Skepticism* (1995) in the winter and was surprised to find him talking of things as direct apprehension of facts. Although it did not seem that Fumerton had gone so far as to embrace Cartesian infallibilism, he was clearly thinking in terms of a robust doctrine of the given. Later, in the spring, I became more interested when I heard Larry BonJour comment on a paper at the Central Division APA meeting. During the course of his comments BonJour made it clear that he had not only abandoned the coherence theory of empirical knowledge but that he now thought he saw how to work out a plausible version of epistemic foundationalism which also relied on a robust doctrine of the given.

Realizing that two of the most talented people working in analytic epistemology seemed to be converging on a very old-fashioned version of foundationalism, and that one of them had built his substantial reputation attacking the given and defending coherentism, I organized a small conference in the winter of 1998 with BonJour and Fumerton as the main speakers. Rather than seeking a commentator who was very much on the other side, I decided instead to seek an advocate of newfangled foundationalism, John Pollock, to comment on both papers. The present volume grew out of that conference. The first two chapters, which are revised versions of the conference papers by Fumerton and BonJour fit together remarkably well. The two do indeed seem to be converging on very similar positions. In addition, Fumerton spends a considerable amount of time setting the scene for the discussion, while BonJour is somewhat more specific, going into more detail about certain matters that Fumerton mentions but does not address in detail. Pollock's comment on the two papers represents a position that is far enough away from Fumerton and BonJour to make for interesting criticism, but not so far away that we get pointless "head butting." The volume is filled out with a second comment on Fumerton and BonJour (and to a much lesser extent Pollock) by Alvin Plantinga, who can also be classified as newfangled foundationalist, and then responses by Fumerton and BonJour. Although the volume is short, I believe it is significant. For one thing, it focuses on articulating, critically examining, and defending a position that philosophers have for the most part either ignored, or mentioned only to abuse, for the last twenty-five or thirty years. Perhaps as significant, the discussion ends up focusing attention on methodological questions regarding the project, or more accurately the projects, epistemologists are pursuing. It may well be that the epistemologists advocate different theories, in this case different versions of foundationalism, because they are pursuing importantly different projects. There are still criticisms to be made of the various theories, but it may be that they are not in competition, that no choice must be made between them.

I should thank several people in closing. The conference this volume grew out of was held at the University of Notre Dame in February 1998 as part of the Philosophy Department's Ernan McMullin Perspectives in Philosophy Series. Mike Loux, The George Shuster Chair, Al Plantinga, The John A. O'Brien Chair in Philosophy, Phil Quinn, The John A. O'Brien Chair in Philosophy, and Peter Van Inwagen, The John Cardinal O'Hara Chair, provided additional support from the endowed chairs they hold. Mike Bergman, Paul Moser and Matthias Steup served as session chairs and enriched the discussions with their participation. Finally, I should thank Paul Moser again, this time for suggesting that the papers and comments from the conference would make a nice little collection.

Notes

1. Obviously, positions and arguments as old as foundationalism and the regress argument have been formulated in very many ways. Many significant distinctions have been drawn and important and subtle observations have been made. It would be foolish, in a few paragraphs of a preface, to try to do justice to this long history.

2. I have already noted that the regress argument and epistemic foundationalism can be formulated in many ways. One might, for example, present them in terms of "knowledge" or "warrant" or "being justified in believing" or "justifying" or "rational belief" or "reasons to believe." These are not merely verbal differences. Different forms of the argument may be more or less good, and the corresponding forms of foundationalism more or less plausible depending upon what sort of epistemic evaluation is at issue. In fact, I believe it becomes fairly clear through the course of the chapters in this volume that the authors of those chapters are focusing on forms of foundationalism that differ in just this way. But in this preface I will formulate the

discussion in terms of "justification," using this as a generic term of positive epistemic evaluation. I want to begin with a very general discussion, and not to focus in on a particular epistemic concept.

3. The qualification is required to include as versions of foundationalism theories that hold some nonfoundational beliefs attain a part of their justification from their connection with basic beliefs and part of their justification from coherence with other nonfoundational beliefs.

Part I

Defending Old-Fashioned Foundationalism

Chapter 1

Classical Foundationalism

Richard Fumerton

It is always hard to tell if a philosophical view is on the rise. However, if one is a proponent of that view, it never hurts to claim that it is, and with the conversion of one of the most prominent coherence theorists to foundationalism,[1] it is as good a time as any to predict a resurgence of the view. My purpose in this paper is to present a kind of overview of what I take to be the main reasons so many epistemologists abandoned classical foundationalism and to sketch the way in which I think one might respond to those concerns. It is always fun to paint with a broad stroke. Due solely to space constraints, of course, one gets to ignore all sorts of views one does not like, fail to defend crucial premises of one's own arguments, and assure one's critics that there are replies to well-known objections not discussed. While I am interested in defending classical foundationalism, there is a sense in which I am skeptical about the project as I have just described it. There are all kinds of radically different epistemological views associated with "classical" foundationalism. Each foundationalist may well band with antifoundationalists in endorsing arguments designed to refute all but the one correct foundationalist view. Indeed my defense of foundationalism will proceed largely by encouraging us to abandon certain well-known versions of the view. Before I am done I will no doubt have antagonized as many foundationalists as antifoundationalists.

Classical Foundationalism

So what makes a version of foundationalism classical? It seems plausible to begin an answer to this question by turning to contemporary internalism/externalism debates in epistemology. Many paradigmatic externalist epistemologies do exemplify a foundationalist structure. Let us say that a foundationalist is someone who claims that there are noninferentially justified beliefs and that all justified beliefs owe their justification ultimately, in part, to the existence of noninferentially justified beliefs. A belief is noninferentially justified if its justification is not constituted by the having of other justified beliefs. This paper was first delivered at Notre Dame, the land of epistemic warrant, and I hasten to add that if you have Plantinga-style reasons for being unhappy with justification as a useful epistemic concept, you can replace reference to justification with reference to knowledge or warrant.[2] Interestingly enough, certain versions of reliabilism and tracking accounts of knowledge are foundationalist views, as we just defined foundationalism. Crude versions of reliabilism will make a distinction between beliefs whose justification depends on the justification of other beliefs, and beliefs whose justification does not. On Goldman's original (1979) view, there are beliefs that are justified in virtue of their being produced by belief-independent, unconditionally reliable processes. These beliefs in turn can be processed by conditionally reliable belief-dependent processes to yield additional justified beliefs. On Nozick's (1981) tracking analysis of knowledge, some beliefs track facts where the tracking mechanism does not involve intermediate beliefs which track facts, and we can view these beliefs as noninferentially justified. As I shall argue later, these versions of foundationalism might recognize the validity of what I call the conceptual regress argument for foundationalism, but I do want to distinguish these views from what I have been calling classical foundationalism. Certainly their proponents thought that they were offering revolutionary alternatives to traditional (foundationalist) epistemology. Shall we define, then, classical foundationalism as foundationalism committed to *internalism*?

I have argued elsewhere (1995) that there is no one straightforward way of understanding the internalism/externalism debate in epistemology. One can distinguish at least the following versions of internalism (and corresponding versions of externalism):

Internal State Internalism

Internal state internalism is the view that S's being justified in believing P is identical with S's being in some internal state—where internal state might be understood as a state of mind consisting of the exemplification of nonrelational properties, or a state of mind consisting of relational properties where the relata are themselves nonrelational properties of mind. While some classical versions of foundationalism, Descartes' for example, might be versions of internal state internalism, there are other traditional foundationalisms, acquaintance theories, for example, which are not in any straightforward way versions of the view. Acquaintance with a fact, object or property is a relation and the state which is S's being acquainted with X may be a state that involves something "outside" of S.[3] As I understand internal state internalism, one must analyze the property of being justified in believing a proposition as an internal state. It is not enough that justification always involves internal states of a subject. Thus, for example, Pollock (1987) claims to be an internal state internalist, but since the very existence of his internalized epistemic norms is to be defined in terms of dispositions to form beliefs under certain circumstances, where these dispositions are made true by factors not internal to the agent, he is not an internal state internalist as I use the term.

Strong Access Internalism

In the empiricist tradition being "in the mind" seems sometimes to have been thought of as being the object of a certain kind of knowledge. There is, then, a natural way of moving from internal state internalism to a view often conflated with it, a view we might call strong access internalism. Strong access internalism is the view that some condition X constitutes S's justification for believing P only if S has or could have access to the fact that X obtains and constitutes S's justification for believing P. If one defines one's access internalism in terms of potential access one can distinguish as many different versions of the view as one can distinguish species of potentiality (and one can distinguish a great many of those).

There are two importantly different versions of strong (actual or potential) access internalism. One is unintelligible; the other merely implausible. If one maintains that for any set of conditions X that one proposes as *constitutive* of S's justification for believing P, those conditions must always be fortified with some other set of conditions describing S's access to X, then the view is hopeless. Call the satisfaction of access conditions to X, A1. Will X together with A1 constitute justification for S to believe P? Not given the view. Our strong access requirements require access (call it A2) to the new proposed sufficient conditions for justification (X and A1). But the conjunction of X, A1, and A2 will not constitute S's justification for believing P as the view requires us to add access to these conditions and so on ad infinitum.

To avoid this problem, the strong access internalist must distinguish carefully a view about what is *constitutive* of justification from a view about what is necessary for justification. If the view is to be intelligible the access internalist must argue that when some set of conditions X constitutes S's justification for believing P, those conditions will be such that they entail that S has access to them. The access, however, need not be part of what constitutes the justification. An analogy might be helpful. P cannot be true unless it is true that P is true—P's truth entails (in some sense of "entails") that it is true that P is true. But it would be a serious mistake to argue that P's being true is constituted by its being true that P is true. The correct analysis of what it is for P to be true should not make reference to metatruths about P's truth even if the correct analysis of P's being true must reveal why P's being true entails that it is true that P is true.

Inferential Internalism

Lying at the heart of many classical foundationalists' concerns with skepticism is a view I call inferential internalism. It is characterized by a principle concerning inferential justification:

(PIJ) To be justified in believing one proposition P on the basis of another E one must be 1) justified in believing E, and 2) justified in believing that E makes probable P.

It is the second clause of the principle of inferential justification that is rejected by all paradigm externalists and that creates enormous difficulties for the philosopher determined to avoid skepticism. Indeed, the aid and comfort it provides the skeptic is often taken by self-proclaimed foundationalists as a reason to reject it. Note that inferential internalism does not entail strong access internalism.

Nonnaturalistic Internalism

It is my own view that paradigm internalists and externalists might usefully be understood as disagreeing over the question of whether one can reduce fundamental epistemic properties to so-called natural properties. Naturalistic epistemologists are convinced that we can ultimately understand epistemic properties of doxastic states in terms of facts about the causal origin of those states. While causal considerations will undoubtedly be invoked by many internalists in characterizing what it is to base one belief on another, their account of the critical notion of noninferential justification is likely to rely on a concept of justification that is not to be defined in terms of contingent facts about how the belief was produced or what the effects of having such beliefs will be.

So what kind of internalism characterizes classical foundationalism? It depends, of course, on one's version of foundationalism. I am leery, however, of supposing that strong access internalism lies at the *heart* of the foundationalism that so dominated the history of philosophy. I have argued that one version of strong access internalism is unintelligible so you will not be surprised by the fact that I am not interested in defending classical foundationalists who are committed to *that* view. In fact, it is difficult to find discussion by the British empiricists (surely almost all paradigmatic foundationalists) of *levels* of knowledge, justification, or rational belief. Hume may have thought that if you know directly some truth then you know that you know it and know that you know that you know it, but I do not know where he says it. Furthermore, depending on one's construal of access or *potential* access, it may be possible for externalists to mimic access requirements for knowledge and justification. If the requirement is only of potential access and the potentiality is understood in terms of logical possibility, I actually cannot imagine a reliabilist, for example, who *should not* allow that whenever one knows or has a justified belief, it is logically possible for one to discover that fact. It is unlikely that a reliabilist would embrace requirements of potential access if the potentiality is understood nomologically, but even if such requirements were accepted by the reliabilist, we would not feel that the view is getting any closer to classical foundationalism if the access in question is analyzed in terms of reliably produced belief. In any event it seems doubtful that people have the causal capacities required to have justified belief if we accept potential access internalism where the potentiality is defined in terms of lawful possibility. The view requires that if I have any justified beliefs, then it is possible for me to have infinitely many, ever increasingly complex beliefs, and speaking for myself, I have difficulty keeping things straight when I try to form the fourth- or fifth-level metabelief.

It is important to note that some very influential arguments against traditional foundationalism, BonJour's (the coherentist) for example, began by embracing some version of strong access internalism and by inviting the foundationalist to defend some version of foundationalism *within the constraints of that view*.[4] I think BonJour's argument was successful against foundationalists who accepted strong access internalism, but, if I am right, his argument is successful against *anyone* who *accepts* strong access internalism, including coherence theorists.[5] The moral, of course, is that one should reject strong access internalism in formulating one's foundationalism.

We have not yet made much progress. We have tentatively suggested that classical foundationalists accept *some* version of internalism, the view that there are noninferentially justified beliefs, and the view that all justified beliefs owe their justification in part ultimately to the existence of these noninferentially justified beliefs. To make further progress, we need to start distinguishing specific versions of traditional foundationalism. Before doing that, however, perhaps we should briefly examine the, historically, most influential argument for foundationalism, the familiar regress argument.

The Regress Argument for Foundationalism

If the only way to be justified in believing one proposition were to justifiably infer it from another, the argument goes, we would face a vicious regress of justification. Invoking the first clause of (PIJ), the foundationalist argues that to be justified in believing P on the basis of E1, one would need to be justified in believing E1, but if the only way to justifiably believe E1 is to infer it from something else E2, we would be then faced with the task of justifiably believing E2, which we could only do by inferring it from something else we justifiably believe E3, and so on ad infinitum. If one is an inferential internalist, the regresses looming are even more intimidating. In addition to justifiably believing E1, we would need to justifiably believe that E1 makes likely P, which we would need to infer from some proposition F1, which we would need to infer from some proposition F2, and so on ad infinitum. We would also need to justifiably believe that F1 makes it likely that E1 makes likely P, which we would need to infer from some G1, which we would need to infer from some G2.... Given inferential internalism there is not one but an infinite number of infinite regresses that seem to threaten our ability to justifiably believe anything, on the supposition that all justification is inferential.

Peter Klein has recently argued in an unpublished paper for a view he calls infinitism. He accepts the first clause of (PIJ) and agrees that it entails that if there are no noninferentially justified beliefs, the existence of a justified belief would entail the existence of an infinite number of justified beliefs, but he goes on to argue that there is nothing vicious about the regress. We can and do have an infinite number of justified dispositional beliefs, enough and of the right sort to allow us to have justified beliefs even if all justification is inferential. He emphasizes that one should not insist that a chain of reasoning actually be completed for a belief to be justified. It is enough that one *is able to* justify each belief in an infinitely complex hierarchy of justification by reference to some other (dispositional) belief in the structure (but not all at once so to speak).

Klein is right that we do have an infinite number of justified beliefs, but I think he misses the real point of the regress argument for noninferentially justified beliefs. The viciousness of the regress is, I believe, *conceptual*. If one tries to analyze or understand the *idea* of inferential justification, one finds oneself inevitably invoking the concept of justification to explain it. To be justified in believing P on the basis of E just *is* in part to be *justified* in believing E. (If the inferential internalist is correct, the justification for believing P on the basis of E is also constituted by the existence of justification to believe that E makes likely P). But so far our analysis of justification in terms solely of inferential justification is blatantly circular. We still need some understanding of what it is for a belief that E to be justified. If one tries to understand having a justified belief that E in terms of its being inferred from something else we *justifiably* believe, we are getting nowhere in our attempt to understand justification. We need some understanding of justification that does not invoke the concept of justification.

I find the following analogy instructive. Suppose a philosopher argues that there is no need for the concept of intrinsic goodness, that we can understand all goodness as instrumental. To say that X is good is always just to say that X produces some Y which is good. Furthermore, we are assured, we must not worry about a regress here, as there is no reason to suppose that there are only a finite number of good things. With an infinite number of good things, there will always be another good thing to make good everything that is good. Would the existence of an infinite number of good things obviate the need to recognize a distinction between intrinsic and instrumental goodness? No it would not. We need the *concept* of intrinsic goodness in order to understand the concept of *instrumental* goodness. We could form no *idea* of instrumental goodness if the only way to understand something's being good was in terms of its leading to something else that is good. In our search for the *conceptual* source of goodness we would always be led to an idea of goodness that was itself defined in terms of an undefined idea of goodness.

In this same way, the infinitist never gives us a noncircular analysis of justification. As an analysis of justification it resembles a recursive definition without a base clause. Unless one can define a concept of justified belief that does not invoke the concept of justified belief, one will have no understanding of the way in which justified "output" depends on *justified* "input."

To escape the conceptual regress argument for foundationalism, one can try to define inferential justification without invoking the concept of justification. Klein's infinitist might try to argue that all we need in order to be inferentially justified in believing P is the ability to produce a nonquestion begging valid argument for P, a nonquestion begging valid argument for the claim that we have produced a sound argument for P, a nonquestion begging valid argument for the claim that we have produced a sound argument for P, and so on ad infinitum. But this cannot be right. I believe P and offer as my evidence for P that God1 believes P and everything God1 believes is true. I am also ready and willing to argue for the soundness of this argument. There is a God2, I claim, who believes that my God1 argument is sound and whatever God2 believes is true. If you want an argument for the soundness of that argument, I have many different infallible Gods in my ontology, each ready to be the subject matter of premises I need to prop up an infinitely complex edifice of beliefs, where the lowest level is supported by everything above. I am confident Klein would not want to allow that one can be justified in believing P through having this system of beliefs, and the reason is that he would never concede that any of the premises in the God arguments were justifiably believed. Inferential justification requires *justified* belief in the relevant premises if the belief in those premises is to yield justified belief in conclusions based on them.

The only other alternative to the foundationalist attempt to end the regress of justification with a concept of noninferentially justified belief is to define some generic concept of justification that has nothing to do with the specific way in which a belief is justified. If, for example, one takes justification to be a fundamentally normative concept and one supposes that one can reduce propositions describing epistemically justified beliefs to propositions describing what one ought to believe, then one might be able to avoid the need to define inferential justification in terms of noninferential justification. But one cannot define epistemic justification in terms of what one ought to believe for reasons that Firth, Plantinga, and others have made clear.[6] And I do not know of any other plausible way to define a generic concept of justification. An externalist coherence theory of justification would do the trick, but BonJour showed us convincingly that coherence to which one has no access (i.e. coherence about which one has no justified belief) is neither here nor there when it comes to producing justified belief. In short I do not think one can define inferential justification except in terms of a kind of justification that is not inferential, and that is why I think one must embrace foundationalism (although not necessarily *internalist* foundationalism).

Traditional Foundationalism and Infallible Belief

But if we reject contemporary externalist epistemologies, how are we to understand this fundamental concept of noninferentially justified belief? One version of internal state internalism seeks to discover foundational knowledge in some characteristic of a belief state. Because Descartes is often thought of as the quintessential foundationalist, it is perhaps not surprising that critics of foundationalism have often been preoccupied with the question of whether or not there are infallible beliefs. It is certainly true that many foundationalists either explicitly or implicitly seemed to endorse the view that we have found the foundations of knowledge and justified belief when we have found beliefs which cannot be mistaken. When Price (1950) introduced his concept of sense-data, knowledge of which would be included in the foundations of empirical knowledge, he contrasted sense-data and their nonrelational properties with other sorts of things about which one could be mistaken, implying that the way to find the correct foundations of knowledge is to scrape away from one's beliefs all that could be false. Following Lehrer (1974) we might formulate the following definition of infallible belief:

(Ia)   S's belief that P at t is infallible if S's believing P at t entails that P is true.

Let us construe the entailment broadly so that P may be said to entail Q if P formally, analytically, or synthetically entails Q.[7]

Although this is a perfectly intelligible definition of infallibility, it is far from clear, as Lehrer argued, that it has much relevance to an attempt to understand the epistemic concept of noninferential *justification*. The problems are familiar and I will not belabor them here. Every necessary truth is entailed by every proposition, and thus if I happen to believe a necessary truth, P, the fact that I believe P will entail that P is true. Thus, by the above definition my belief that P will be infallible whenever P is a necessary truth even if I believe P solely on a whim. Surely this concept of infallibility has precious little to do with whether or not my belief is justified. If we restrict our attention to contingent propositions one can still give examples of propositions entailed by the fact that they are believed even when the person who believes the proposition does not "see" the entailment and, therefore, lacks justification.[8]

To deal with this problem one could tinker with the definition of infallible belief, but once one sees that mere entailment between the having of a belief and the truth of what is believed does not provide justification, perhaps we should look elsewhere for the foundations of knowledge and justified belief. By doing so we may be able to avoid a host of standard objections to foundationalism. Although one can give a few examples of contingent propositions whose truth is trivially entailed by their being believed, critics of infallible-belief foundationalism have argued that there are simply not enough infallible beliefs upon which to support the edifice of justified beliefs we are trying to erect. Thus we remember philosophers employing thought experiments in an attempt to convince Cartesian foundationalists that their favorite candidates for infallible beliefs were not infallible at all. Armstrong (1963) imagined us in a future characterized by a utopian neurophysiology. We are wired to complex machines that inform us that, despite the fact that we believe we are in pain, there is simply no indication of the sort of neural activity associated with pain. Might it not be reasonable in such a situation to conclude that we simply have a false belief that we are in pain?[9] Lehrer (1974) argued that one can genuinely (as opposed to merely verbally) confuse pains with itches and for that reason arrive at a false belief that one is in pain. In his contribution to this volume, Pollock warns of the ways in which we can easily make mistakes in trying to characterize our own experience.

Whatever the force of these specific thought experiments, there is a very general argument designed to establish that the foundationalist's favorite candidates for noninferentially justified empirical beliefs are not infallible. It is a Humean sort of argument that proceeds from the simple observation that in the vast majority of cases, the belief that P is one state of affairs and P's being the case is a different state of affairs. If these really are two distinct facts, then why could not one have the one without the other?[10] Although it does not add much to the logical force of the argument, one can again employ our hunches about how the brain might work to rhetorically bolster the argument. Consider again a standard candidate for an infallible empirical belief, my belief that I am in pain now, for example. It is surely *possible* that the region of the brain causally responsible for producing the belief that I am in pain is entirely different from the region of the brain causally responsible for producing the pain. There may be a causal connection between the occurrence of the "pain" brain event and the occurrence of the "belief" brain event, or vice versa, but even if the causal connection holds it will be a contingent fact that it does. It hardly seems that the neurophysiologist could discover these (or any other) causal connections purely a priori. But if the brain state responsible for my belief that I am in pain is wholly different from the brain state responsible for the pain, then it is in principle possible to produce the one without the other. The belief will not *entail* the truth of what is believed.

Infallible *Justification*

The foregoing argument has a great deal of plausibility, I think, and in any event it has always seemed strange to me to search for foundations in mere *belief*. What justifies me in believing that I am in pain? The mere fact that I believe that I am in pain? Well what *is* it about this belief that makes it so different from other beliefs? Why does my belief that I am in pain constitute a kind of justification, but my belief that there are ghosts does not constitute a kind of justification? The appeal to belief as a justifier borders on a non sequitur if one is genuinely attempting to find a useful characterization of a special kind of epistemic relation one can bear to *truth* that obviates the need for inference.

As BonJour (the coherentist) pointed out, this same lack of a genuine response seems to characterize those foundationalists who seek to identify the source of noninferential justification with the fact that makes the noninferentially justified belief true.[11] When asked what justifies one in believing that one is in pain, this foundationalist identifies the pain itself. But what is it about the pain that makes it a justifier? When you believe that I am in pain, my pain does not justify you in believing that I am in pain (according to most foundationalists), so there must be something different about my relationship to my pain that enters into the account of what constitutes the justification.[12] It is the fact that I have a kind of *access* to my pain that you do not have that makes my belief noninferentially justified while you must rely on inference. One still needs an account of what this relation is, but before we consider such an account it is worth noting that we could have defined the concept of infallibility in a way that makes it potentially more useful in developing a foundationalist theory of justification. The relevant question is not whether my belief entails the truth of what is believed. It is, rather, whether my *justification* entails the truth of what is believed:

(Ib)   S's belief that P at t is infallible if S's justification for believing P at t relevantly entails the truth of P.

It is necessary to qualify the entailment as relevant to circumvent the problems already discussed in connection with Ia. Whenever I have any justification at all for believing a proposition that turns out to be necessarily true, that justification will entail the necessary truth. But we do not want just any sort of justification to yield infallibly justified belief even if the object of that belief is a necessary truth. What is the difference between relevant and irrelevant entailment? This question is notoriously difficult to answer, but intuitively it should have something to do with the fact that would make true the proposition entailed and the fact that would make true the proposition that entails it. More specifically, we could say that P relevantly entails Q only if the fact that would make P true is at least a constituent of the fact that would make Q true. This suggestion can be considered at best only preliminary, since we will obviously need a more detailed account of facts and their constituents. That I have gray hair entails that someone has gray hair, but is my having gray hair a constituent of the fact that someone has gray hair? There is certainly a sense in which it is something one can point to in answer to the question "What makes it true that someone has gray hair?" One cannot appropriately point to my having gray hair as something that makes it true that two plus two equals four.

Acquaintance and Noninferential Justification

I have suggested that neither a belief nor the fact that makes true what is believed is by itself a plausible justification at all, let alone the kind of justification that might end a regress of justification. Rather, we must stand in some sort of special *relation* to the truth of what is believed, or more precisely, we must stand in some sort of special relation to the fact that makes true what we believe. I have argued elsewhere (1995) that the most fundamental concept required to make sense of traditional foundationalism is the concept of acquaintance.[13] In order to explain my acquaintance theory of noninferential justification, however, I must digress and sketch a highly controversial theory of truth and intentionality.

I take the primary bearers of truth-value to be thoughts (which I also refer to as propositions). The secondary bearers of truth-value are the linguistic items that express them. Thoughts I take to be nonrelational properties of a mind or self. True thoughts correspond to or "picture" facts. False thoughts fail to correspond. A fact is a nonlinguistic complex that consists of an entity's or entities' exemplifying properties. The world contained facts long before it contained minds and thoughts. Unless there are uninstantiated universals, however, in one perfectly clear sense the world might have contained no truths before there were conscious beings, for without conscious beings there would be no bearers of truth-value.[14] There were facts that would have made true the relevant thoughts had they existed, and by employing counterfactuals we can make good sense of such commonplace assertions as that it was true hundreds of millions of years ago that there were no conscious beings.

On my view every intentional state *is* a thought. Believing that there are ghosts and fearing that their are ghosts are *species* of the same thought that there are ghosts. We can represent true and false belief respectively as follows:

S believes truly that P when S exemplifies the property of thinking (in a belief mode) that P and there is some x such that the thought that P corresponds to x.

S believes falsely that P when S exemplifies the property of thinking that P (in a belief mode) and there is no x such that the thought that P corresponds to x.

The above correspondence theory of truth avoids the need for such ontological nightmares as nonexistent states of affairs to serve as the "objects" of false beliefs, and it preserves a much more natural way of understanding the *referents* of sentences, analogous to the referents of names and definite descriptions. Unlike Frege, we have no need for such mysteries as The True and The False to serve as the referents of true and false sentences, respectively. Rather, we adopt the more straightforward view that just as the successful use of a name refers to an individual, so the successful—that is true—attempt to refer to the world with a descriptive sentence succeeds in picking out a fact. Some names, such as "Pegasus," do not succeed in referring to any individual, and some sentences, like "Dogs have eight legs," do not refer to any fact. Direct theories of reference aside, having a referent is not necessary for having meaning, and the thoughts that false sentences express give those sentences meaning despite the fact that they fail to refer.

Acquaintance is *not* another intentional state to be construed as a nonrelational property of the mind. Acquaintance is a sui generis *relation* that holds between a self and a thing, property, or fact. To be acquainted with a fact is not *by itself* to have any kind of propositional knowledge or justified belief, and for that reason I would prefer not to use the old terminology of knowledge by acquaintance. One can be acquainted with a property or fact without even possessing the conceptual resources to *represent* that fact in thought, and certainly without possessing the ability to linguistically express that fact. But if this is true, what has acquaintance got to do with epistemology?

In one of the most influential arguments against foundationalism, Sellars argued that the idea of the given in traditional epistemology contains irreconcilable tensions. On the one hand, to ensure that something's being given does not involve any other beliefs, proponents of the view want it to be untainted by the application of *concepts*. The kinds of data that are given to us are also presumably given in sense experience to all sorts of other creatures. On the other hand, the whole doctrine of the given is designed to end the regress of justification, to give us secure foundations for the rest of what we justifiably infer from the given. But to make sense of making inferences from the given, the given would have to be propositional. Minimally, the given must have a truth-value. But the kind of thing that has a truth-value involves the application of concepts or thought, a capacity not possessed by at least lower-order animals.[15]

The solution to the dilemma presented by Sellars and others is to reemphasize that acquaintance is not *by itself* an epistemic relation. Acquaintance is a relation that other animals probably bear to properties and even facts, but it also probably does not give these animals any kind of justification for believing anything, precisely because these other animals probably do not have beliefs. Without *thought* there is no truth, and without a bearer of truth-value there is nothing to be justified or unjustified. But how does acquaintance give us noninferential justification? My suggestion is that one has a noninferential justification for believing P when one has the thought that P and one is acquainted with the fact that P, the thought that P, *and* the fact which is the thought that P's *corresponding* to the fact that P. No single act of acquaintance yields knowledge or justified belief, but when one has the relevant thought, the three acts together constitute noninferential justification. When everything that is *constitutive* of a thought's being true is immediately before consciousness, there is nothing more that one could want or need to justify a belief.[16] The state that constitutes noninferential justification is a state that contains as constituents both the bearer of truth-value and the truth-maker.

The reader might well complain that if mere acquaintance with a fact does not constitute an epistemic property, surely one cannot conjure up an epistemic property by multiplying acts of acquaintance. But if this is intended to be a formal objection to the view I presented, it involves committing the fallacy of division. Because none of the components of a complex state of affairs constitutes the exemplification of an epistemic property, it does not follow that the complex does not constitute the exemplification of such a property. Classical acquaintance theorists like Russell appropriately emphasized the role of acquaintance with particulars, properties, and even facts in grounding justification. But a fact is not a truth, and what one needs to end a regress of justification is a direct confrontation with *truth*. To secure that confrontation, one needs to be directly aware of not just a truth-maker (a fact to which a truth corresponds) but also a truth-bearer (a thought) and the correspondence that holds between them.

Because the relations of acquaintance and correspondence that the above account appeals to are sui generis, there is precious little one can say by way of trying to explain the concept to one who claims not to understand it. Because acquaintance is not like any other relation, there is no useful genus under which to subsume it. One can give examples of facts with which one is acquainted and in this way present a kind of "ostensive" definition of acquaintance, but philosophers who think the concept is gibberish are unlikely to find themselves acquainted with their being acquainted with various facts. When one is acquainted with a fact, the fact is *there* before consciousness. Nothing stands "between" the self and the fact. But these are metaphors and in the end are as likely to be misleading as helpful. As I indicated, one can try to ostend through thought experiment the relation of being directly aware of something. To take a familiar example, think of the way in which one can become engrossed in a conversation and temporarily fail to notice the back pain from which one is suffering. Some philosophers will insist, of course, that the pain has simply disappeared. It seems more plausible to me, however, to suppose that the pain existed all along, but that for a brief period of time one simply was not aware of it. It is that awareness which was present, absent, and then present again, which is the direct awareness about which I have been talking.

Correspondence, too, is sometimes thought of as a picturing relation, but the picturing metaphor is largely responsible for the caricature of the view one so often encounters in the cruder theories of "ideas" as pale copies of reality. It is tempting to at least mention the metaphor of a Kodak print and the scene it depicts as a way of explaining the relation that a true thought bears to the fact with which it corresponds, but most thoughts are not "pictures" and the relation of correspondence has nothing to do with any kind of similarity that holds between the thought and the fact it represents. Correspondence is not like anything else; it cannot be informatively subsumed under a genus, and it cannot be analyzed into any less problematic concepts.

Is acquaintance a source of infallible justification? The answer is in one sense straightforward. If my being acquainted with the fact that P is part of what justifies me in believing P and if acquaintance is a genuine relation that requires the existence of its relata, then when I am acquainted with the fact that P, P is true. The fact I am acquainted with is the very fact that makes P true. The very source of justification includes that which makes true the belief. In a way it is this idea that makes an acquaintance foundation theory so attractive. I have no need to turn to other beliefs to justify my belief that I am in pain because the very fact that makes the belief true is unproblematically before consciousness, as is the correspondence that holds between my thought and the fact. Again, everything one could possibly want or need by way of justification is there in consciousness.

Notice that the infallibility of the justification provided by acquaintance is due to the presence of the fact itself as a constituent of the justifier. It is interesting to note that in this respect there are remarkable similarities between this classic version of foundationalism and at least some paradigmatic externalist views. On certain causal theories of direct knowledge, for example, my belief that P is justified by its being caused in the appropriate way by the fact that P, the very fact that makes my belief true. If a causal relationship between the fact that P and my belief that P were a kind of justification, then that justification too would be infallible. Its existence would, trivially, entail the truth of what I believe. From the fact that a certain justification is infallible, it does *not* follow that one could not mistakenly believe that one has an infallibly justified belief. Certainly the causal theory I have just sketched would have no difficulty allowing for a person who mistakenly concluded that his belief that P was caused by the fact that P, and if the causal theory were correct, that person could mistakenly infer that the justification in support of his belief entailed the truth of what he believed. Similarly, I think that it is in principle possible for a person to mistakenly conclude that he is acquainted with something actually known only through inference. One might trust a philosopher with a mistaken epistemology, for example, and falsely, perhaps even justifiably, believe that one is acquainted with a fact when one is not. Although this complicates matters considerably, I also argue that it may be possible on an acquaintance theory to have noninferential justification that does not entail the truth of what is believed. Specifically, I have argued that one might be acquainted with a fact very similar to the fact that makes P true, and such acquaintance might give one a justified but false belief that P. It should be clear that this admission is perfectly compatible with the rather trivial claim that when one's justification for believing P consists in part in being acquainted with the fact that P, that justification is infallible in that it entails the truth of P.

The above discussion emphasizes that one must be cautious in appealing to the possibility of error by way of ruling out acquaintance with various sorts of phenomena. Nevertheless, arguments from the possibility of error still have a role to play in deciding with what we can be directly acquainted. If one concedes, for example, that the *justification* one has now for believing that there is a table before one is perfectly compatible with the table's not being there, then one has just conceded that one is not directly acquainted with the table. It seems to me that traditional arguments from the possibility of hallucination *do* establish that one cannot be directly acquainted with any facts about the external world. If one compares the justification one has for believing some proposition about the external world with the justification one would have were one suffering from some vivid hallucinatory experience, it does seem obvious to me that the justification would be the same in both cases. In hallucinatory experience the justification cannot be acquaintance with the external object, so it cannot be such acquaintance in the case of veridical experience. It is true that one can formally respond to the argument by denying the crucial premise—that the justification in both cases is the same. Clearly it can not be the same, one might argue, for in veridical experience one is directly aware of a physical object, whereas in hallucinatory experience one is not. At this point, however, one probably has no recourse but to make a phenomenological appeal—is it not just obvious upon "inspection" that the two evidential situations are the same? Such an appeal, however, is just a disguised way of making reference to one's acquaintance with one's evidence, and in the end one cannot avoid appeals to what one is acquainted with in order to decide with what one is acquainted.

If I am asked what reason I have for thinking that there is such a relation as acquaintance, I will give the unhelpful answer that I am acquainted with such a relation. The answer is question-begging if it is designed to convince someone that there is such a relation, but if the view is true it would be unreasonable to expect its proponent to give any other answer. I can also raise dialectical considerations and object to alternatives. One of the dialectical advantages of the above view is that it can easily respond to some of the classic arguments against the existence of noninferentially justified belief.

One of the most discussed arguments against foundationalism again focuses on concepts. There is no truth-value without concept application, the argument goes. But to apply a concept is to make a judgment about class membership, and to make a judgment about class membership always involves relating the thing about which the judgment is made to other paradigm members of the class. These judgments of relevant similarity will minimally involve beliefs about the past, and thus be inferential in character. Our reply to the argument is straightforward. To make a judgment, say that this is red, involves having the thought that this is red, but the thought does not involve relating this to some other thing. Indeed, it is in principle possible to produce a thought of red in the mind of someone who has never experienced a red thing. Since language is only a secondary and conventional means of representation, it goes without saying that the inferential character of our judgments concerning the linguistically correct way to express a thought are neither here nor there when it comes to the question of whether the thought expressed can be noninferentially justified.

The intelligibility of the above account does rest on the intelligibility of a world that has structure independent of any structure imposed by the mind. Without nonlinguistic facts that are independent of the thoughts that represent them, one could not make sense of a relation of acquaintance between a self and a fact, a relation that grounds direct knowledge. Indeed, I suspect that it is concern with this idea that lies at the heart of much dissatisfaction with traditional foundationalism. Since Kant there has always been a strong undercurrent of antirealism running through philosophy. The metaphor again is that of the mind imposing a structure on reality. And there is an intuitively plausible sense in which one can genuinely wonder whether it makes sense to ask about the number of colors that are exemplified in the world independently of some framework provided by color concepts. But despite the periodic popularity of extreme nominalism and antirealism, it is surely absurd to suppose that it is even in principle possible for a mind to force a structure on a *literally* unstructured world. There are indefinitely many ways to sort the books in a library and some are just as useful as others, but there would be no way to begin sorting books were books undifferentiated. The world comes to us with its differences. Indeed, it comes to us with far too many differences for us to be bothered noticing all of them. And it is in this sense that the mind *does* impose order on chaos. Thought is abstract in the sense that many different actual properties can all correspond to a single thought of red. And it is up to us how finely we want to draw our color concepts. Although I understand that the empirical evidence is at best questionable, it is common for philosophers to call our attention to the alleged fact that some cultures have far more finely grained color concepts than our culture. If one distinguishes color concepts from linguistic terms to express those concepts, the empirical claim is difficult to assess, but one must surely admit that the alleged phenomenon is in principle possible. Given the above framework for understanding thought and truth, there would be a sense in which the one culture would entertain truths about colors that the other culture would be causally unable to accept. But the fact that there is good sense to be made of the relativity of conceptual frameworks should not mislead one into thinking that the determinate properties exemplified in the world depend for their existence on concepts.

I have presented at length a view that I take to be the most plausible version of classical foundationalism. In what sense, if any, is it internalist? Well, on the specific version of the view I defended, thought is an internal property of the mind, if by "internal" one means "nonrelational." The crucial concepts of acquaintance and correspondence, however, are relational. It is true that given my own views in normative epistemology, it turns out that the only contingent facts with which we are acquainted are mental states or features of mental states. When one has noninferential justification for believing a contingent proposition, the relevant acts of acquaintance will involve constituents, all of which are "internal" to the subject. It would be nice if we could be acquainted with facts about the external world, but in my view such facts always outstrip anything before our minds. Facts about physical objects and their properties are complex facts about the existence of "permanent possibilities" of sensations, and the relevant subjunctives we use to describe these possibilities are made true, in part, by lawful regularities of a kind that preclude being before consciousness. One realizes as soon as one understands the content of claims about the physical world that it simply is not true that everything relevant to their truth is there before consciousness to be "inspected."[17]

But even if I am myself sympathetic to the view that noninferentially justified empirical beliefs end with the content of our minds, it should be emphasized that the *metaepistemological* acquaintance theory of noninferential justification does not by itself entail any position with respect to what might be the objects of acquaintance. In previous discussion of the attempt to define internalism in terms of internal states being sufficient for justification, I noted that one might be a sense-datum theorist who thinks one can be directly acquainted with the fact that the surface of a physical object exemplifies a certain property. One might think that there are mind-independent universals and claim to be acquainted with them. One might think that there are mind-independent, nonoccurrent states of affairs and claim to be acquainted with logical relations that hold between them. It is at best unclear as to whether or not any of the above acts of acquaintance should be called internal states, and thus equally unclear as to whether a foundationalism defined using the concept of acquaintance is always going to be a species of "internal state" internalism.

As we saw earlier, being internal might also be understood in terms of access. Does an acquaintance theory hold that when one is noninferentially justified in believing P one has access to, that is, knowledge or justified belief about, the fact that one has such justification? No. But as we saw earlier it is good that the answer is "No." In the paradigm case, I am noninferentially justified in believing P when I have the thought that P and am simultaneously acquainted with the thought that P, the fact that P, and the relation of correspondence holding between them. To have noninferential justification for believing that I am noninferentially justified in believing P, I must have that rather complex thought and simultaneously be acquainted with its correspondence to an equally complex fact. And for me to be noninferentially justified in believing that I am noninferentially justified in believing that I am noninferentially justified in believing that P, I must be acquainted with facts so complex as to boggle my poor consciousness. The position that in order to have a noninferentially justified belief on an acquaintance theory one *must* be noninferentially justified in believing that one has such justification invites a vicious regress of infinitely many, increasingly complex conscious states.

If acquaintance foundationalism is neither a form of internal state internalism nor strong access internalism, why call it internalism at all? The answer I suggested earlier points to its reliance on the sui generis concept of acquaintance that is fundamental to epistemology and that cannot be reduced to nonepistemic concepts, particularly the nomological concepts upon which all externalists build their analyses.

Foundationalism and Skepticism

Many critics of traditional foundationalism will no doubt be delighted if a defense of foundationalism turns on a defense of the acquaintance theory sketched above, replete with its unfashionable ontological commitments. A detailed defense of foundationalism, however, requires a detailed foundationalist view. I want to close, however, by at least mentioning another reason so many philosophers abandoned foundationalism, one that has very little to do with the intrinsic plausibility of an account of noninferential justification. It has long been clear to

me that the primary reservations many antifoundationalists have with foundationalism, particularly foundationalism coupled with inferential internalism, is
their conviction that the view will inevitably lead to skepticism. This is really
the subject of an entirely different talk—one I considered giving. Since I did not
give it, I have time only for a short answer to the objection that traditional foundationalism leads to skepticism. The answer is that it probably does, but that it
is a matter of considerable philosophical hubris to reject an epistemological view
for that reason. If we had the time, I would try to convince you that the principle
of inferential justification states standards of justification that are reflected in all
kinds of commonplace inquiries. One cannot simply reject it because we cannot
figure out how to secure noninferential knowledge of probabilistic connections at
those fundamental levels where our habits of inference are unreflective—the levels at which philosophical inquiry begins. But epistemology is a distinctly philosophical enterprise. We are asking odd questions because they are so fundamental and we are insisting on rigorous standards for what constitutes an acceptable
answer to these questions. In commonplace inquiries we simply assume knowledge of the past based on memory, the future based on inductive inference, the
external world based on perception. The question is whether we can move from
this data to other conclusions employing inferences we give ourselves as legitimate. When we start doing philosophy, we stop getting gifts. We must justify
what we normally do not bother to justify and it may not be possible to do it.
To paraphrase Hume, it may be that nature has been wise enough not to leave
our ability to form beliefs about the world around us to "uncertain" reason.

Notes

A version of this paper was read at a Notre Dame epistemology conference. I would
like to thank the many participants in that conference, faculty and graduate students,
for their helpful comments and criticisms. I would particularly like to thank Michael
DePaul, Laurence BonJour, John Pollock, Alvin Plantinga, Michael Kremer, Michael
Bergmann, Marian David, and Paul Moser.

1. I refer to Laurence BonJour. See his paper in this volume.
2. Plantinga presents these reasons in Plantinga (1988, 1992, 1993a & 1993b).
3. While many acquaintance theorists held that one is only acquainted with one's
internal states, there is nothing in the view that precludes the possibility of being
acquainted with external objects, surfaces of objects, for example. Moore certainly
toyed with the idea of taking sense-data to be mind-independent entities with which
we can nevertheless be acquainted. Bergmann (1964) specifically endorsed such a
view.
4. BonJour (1985). As will be evident from his paper contained in this volume,
BonJour, the coherentist, is no more. I will, however, still be referring to some of his
earlier arguments which he now disavows, and when I do I will refer to him as
BonJour, the coherentist.
5. An argument I make in some detail in Fumerton (1995): Chapter 5.
6. See Firth (1959) and Plantinga (1988, 1992, 1993a & 1993b).
7. Let us say that P formally entails Q if it is a tautology that if P then Q; P analytically entails Q when the proposition that if P then Q can be turned into a tautology through the substitution of synonymous expressions; P synthetically entails Q

when the proposition that if P then Q is true in all possible worlds but is neither a tautology nor an analytic truth. It should go without saying that these are sketches, not satisfactory analyses of these problematic philosophical concepts.

8. For more detailed examples see Lehrer (1990) and Goldman (1979).

9. The answer seems to me to be a resounding "No." My concern here, however, is simply to remind of some of the arguments that have been raised in connection with this issue.

10. Ayer presents this argument (1956): 19.

11. See BonJour (1985): 58-78.

12. In his contribution to this volume, BonJour now seems to be willing to claim that it is the fact of being in pain that constitutes justification for believing that one is in pain. I am not sure, however, that he and I in the end disagree. He defines con-scious pain as pain one is aware of, and I have no objection to introducing this as technical vocabulary. The key question is whether it is the awareness of the pain, something that is distinct from what one is aware of, that is providing the justification.

13. My views there and here are obviously influenced to a great extent by Russell. Probably the closest Russell ever comes to endorsing a view like mine is in Russell (1984), particularly Chapter VI. My thanks to Michael Kremer for directing me to critical passages.

14. Plantinga has warned me, with good reason, that I should try very hard to find room in my ontology for universals. With them, I could take the property (universal) of thinking that P as the bearer of truth-value and save myself no end of grief. Unin-stantiated universals (like propositions as traditionally conceived) necessarily exist. Intuitively, one does not want it to be a necessary truth that there are thoughts, but if the bearers of truth-value are contingent thoughts then in all possible worlds in which there are truth-bearers it will be true that there are thoughts. The easiest phi-losophical position to defend is not always the truth, however, and I am still strug-gling to get by without an ontology of universals.

15. This argument is given in Sellars (1963): 131-32, and also in BonJour (1985): Chapter 4.

16. In an earlier version of this paper, I claimed that the acts of acquaintance en-tailed that the relevant belief was justified. As Paul Moser reminded me at the Notre Dame conference, however, I do not want to say *that* if we allow, as we probably should, that the belief must be *based* on the relevant acts of acquaintance. For that reason I try to more carefully state the thesis as one about the existence of justifica-tion rather than as one about sufficient conditions for justified belief.

17. As I suggested earlier, one might be able to reach this same conclusion by employing an argument from the possibility of hallucination. That argument, as we saw, rests on the claim that we have the same justification in both hallucinatory and veridical experience for believing what we do about the external world. Whether or not one can present a plausible way of rejecting that premise (given the phenome-nological evidence) will ultimately rest in part on one's ontological analysis of physical objects and their relations to perceptions.

Chapter 2

Toward a Defense of Empirical Foundationalism

Laurence BonJour

My aim in this paper is to take some initial steps toward the development and defense of a quite traditional foundationalist view of the justification of empirical beliefs and in particular of beliefs about physical objects: the view that such justification depends ultimately on basic or foundational beliefs about the contents of sensory experience. I say "justification" rather than "knowledge," because I want to sidestep issues about whether justification is a requirement for knowledge and about the, to my mind, rather vexed concept of knowledge itself. My concern is thus with what reasons there are for thinking that our familiar beliefs about the physical world are true, where I have in mind reasons: (i) that do not in some way beg the question by presupposing the acceptability of other beliefs about physical objects; and (ii) that are in principle available through reflection and analysis to believers more or less like ourselves. (But I will not be very concerned with the question of whether the justification in question is actually in the minds of ordinary people.) It is to this question that I now think that a traditional foundationalism offers the only hope of a nonskeptical answer.

Until roughly forty years ago, such a foundationalist view was generally acknowledged as obviously correct and indeed as more or less the only serious epistemological alternative to a pervasive skepticism. In the intervening period, however, empirical foundationalism of this sort, or indeed of any sort, has been subjected to incessant attack and has come to be widely regarded as an obviously untenable and even hopeless view. As a result, a very substantial proportion of the epistemological work in this period has been aimed at the delineation and development of nonskeptical alternatives to empirical foundationalism. This effort has spawned various widely discussed views, such as coherentism, contextualism, externalism, and a variety of others that are less easily labeled. (Though externalism can be regarded as a version of foundationalism, it rejects the internalist requirement, common to all traditional versions of foundationalism, that the justification for a belief must be cognitively accessible to the believer. My concern here is to defend a foundationalist view of the more traditional, internalist sort, and it is such a view that subsequent uses of the term "foundationalism" should be taken to refer to.)

I myself have played a role in these developments, offering some of the arguments against foundationalism and attempting to develop and defend the coherentist alternative in particular. But having labored long in the intriguing but ultimately barren labyrinths of coherentism, I have come to the conviction that the recent antifoundationalist trend is a serious mistake, one that is taking epistemological inquiry in largely the wrong direction and giving undeserved credibility to those who would reject epistemology altogether.

I have two main reasons for this conviction. One, which can only be briefly touched on here, is that none of the recent alternatives seem to me to succeed in providing a genuinely nonskeptical alternative to traditional foundationalism or to have any serious prospect of doing so. Of the main alternatives, contextualism and externalism concede more or less openly that we do not in general have internally accessible, nonquestion-begging reasons for thinking that our beliefs about the world are true, a result that seems to me to constitute in itself a very deep and intuitively quite implausible version of skepticism. And coherentism, despite my efforts and those of others to avoid such a fate (efforts that in retrospect seem rather obviously desperate), now seems to me to lead inexorably to the same dismal result—largely, as many have long argued, because of the problem of access to one's own system of beliefs.[1]

The second reason, elaborated below, is that I now think that I can see a way to develop a foundationalist position that avoids the objections to such a view that seem to me most important. I should make clear at the outset, however, that I will be concerned here almost exclusively with objections that challenge the possibility or availability of the foundational beliefs themselves. There is, of course, a second main problem that any foundationalist must face: that of whether and how it is possible to infer in an adequately justified way from the foundational beliefs to nonfoundational beliefs and especially to beliefs about the physical world.[2] This problem, as discussion of the "problem of the external world" extending at least back to Descartes make clear, is very serious. But it does not seem to me to provide in itself a clear basis for an objection to foundationalism until and unless some alternative view does better in this respect—and does so without construing justification (or knowledge) in ways that amount to the tacit acceptance of serious versions of skepticism. For this reason, and also for lack of space and very likely, for the present at least, of adequate wit, I will leave this second main problem largely untouched on the present occasion, saying only a little about it at the very end of the paper.

I. Foundationalism and a Central Objection

I begin with a closer examination of the central concept of a basic or foundational belief. This will lead to one of the main objections to empirical foundationalism, in relation to which the specific account of the foundational beliefs to be offered here will be developed.

As reflected in the familiar epistemic regress argument for empirical foundationalism, which I will not take the time to rehearse here, a foundational or "basic" belief is supposed to be an empirical belief that (a) is adequately justified in the epistemic sense, but (b) whose epistemic justification does not depend on inference from further empirical beliefs that would in turn have to be somehow justified. The main problem is to understand how these two elements can be successfully combined. To say that such a foundational belief is epistemically justified is to say that there is some sort of reason or basis or warrant for thinking that it is true or at least likely to be true—one, I will assume here, that is available or accessible to the person in question. But this reason or basis or warrant is not supposed to take the form of a further empirical belief, for example, a belief that the belief originally in question has some feature that can be independently shown to be indicative of truth.[3] What form then does it take?

It is sometimes suggested that the basic or foundational beliefs are either "self-justifying" or else "not in need of justification," but both of these formulations seem to me to render the epistemic status of such beliefs needlessly problematic and even paradoxical. A basic belief cannot literally be self-justifying unless the foundationalist accepts circular reasoning as a source of justification, a view that seems obviously unacceptable (and that would also undercut one main objection to coherentism). Nor can it be plausibly claimed that the foundational beliefs are self-evident in the sense that is sometimes claimed to apply to beliefs justified a priori: the content of an empirical, contingent belief cannot by itself provide a good reason for thinking that it is true.[4] And the only way that a belief that is to serve as a foundation for other beliefs can itself be "not in need of justification" is if it already possesses something tantamount to justification (whether or not that term is employed), in which case this status needs to be further explained.

Here the obvious and, I now believe, correct thing to say is that basic or foundational beliefs are justified by appeal to *experience*. But the difficulty, which turns out to be very formidable, is to give a clear and dialectically perspicuous picture of how this is supposed to work.

Foundationalists such as C. I. Lewis and Richard Fumerton,[5] among many others, have spoken at this point of the "direct apprehension" of or "direct acquaintance" with the relevant experiential content. Contrary to my own earlier arguments,[6] I now believe that there is a way to understand such formulations that leads to a defensible view. On the surface, however, this answer is seriously problematic in the following way. The picture it suggests is that in a situation of foundational belief there are two distinguishable elements, in addition to the relevant sensory experience itself. First, there is an allegedly basic or foundational belief whose content pertains to some aspect of that experience. Second, there is what appears to be a second, independent mental act, an act of direct apprehension of or direct acquaintance with the relevant experiential feature. And it is, of course, this second act that is supposed to supply the person's reason for thinking that the belief is true.

But the problem now is to understand the nature and epistemic status of this second mental act itself. If it is construed as cognitive and conceptual, having as its content something like the proposition or claim that the experience in question has the specific character indicated by the belief, then it is easy to see how this second mental act can, if it *is itself justified*, provide a reason for thinking that the belief is true, but hard to see why it does not itself require justification of some further sort, some reason for thinking that its propositional or assertive content is true or correct. And to say simply that acts of direct apprehension, unlike ordinary beliefs, somehow cannot by their very nature be mistaken is to stipulate that the problem does not exist without offering any clear explanation of how and why this is so.

If, on the other hand, the mental act of direct apprehension or direct acquaintance is construed as noncognitive and nonconceptual in character, as not involving any propositional claim about the character of the experience, then while no further issue of justification is apparently raised, it becomes difficult to see how such an act of direct apprehension can provide any reason or other basis for thinking that the original allegedly foundational belief is true. If one who is directly acquainted with an experience is not thereby propositionally aware that it has such-and-such features, in what way is his belief that he has an experience with those features justified by the act of direct acquaintance?

It is this dilemma[7] that has always seemed to me to be the most fundamental objection to empirical foundationalism, and the core of the present paper will be an account of how it can be answered. I will begin in the next two sections by considering the somewhat tangential but more easily accessible case of the justification of a metabelief about a conscious, occurrent first-order belief or assertive thought, and then turn in the following section to the main issue of the justification of beliefs about sensory experience.

II. Foundational Beliefs about One's Own Beliefs

As I work on this paper, I believe that I am having various occurrent beliefs or assertive thoughts about foundationalism and its problems. For example, I believe that I presently have the occurrent belief or thought that foundationalism is much more defensible than most philosophers think. What is my justification for this second-order metabelief (assuming that there is any)?

As already indicated, the natural answer to this question, which is also the one that I want to elaborate and defend here, is to appeal to the conscious *experience* involved in having the occurrent belief or thought in question. But it is crucial for present purposes that the nature and status of this experience be understood in the right way. My suggestion is that an intrinsic and essential aspect of having an occurrent belief is being consciously aware of the two correlative aspects of its content: first, its propositional content, in this case the proposition that foundationalism is much more defensible than most philosophers think; and, second, the assertory rather than, for example, questioning character of one's entertaining of that content. These two awarenesses (or rather two aspects of one awareness) are, I am suggesting, not apperceptive or reflective in character: they do not involve a second-order mental act with the propositional content that I have the belief in question. Instead, they are *constitutive* of the first-level state of belief itself in that they are what make it the very belief that it is, rather than some other belief or a different sort of conscious state altogether. The point here is simply that occurrent belief or thought is, after all, a *conscious* state, and that what one is primarily conscious of in having such a belief is precisely its propositional and assertive content; not to be consciously aware of that content would be not to have the conscious, occurrent belief at all.

It is this account of the experiential aspect of occurrent belief that seems to me to allow an escape between the horns of the antifoundationalist dilemma posed in the previous section. The crucial point is that the most fundamental experience involved in having an occurrent belief is *neither* a second-order apperceptive or reflective awareness that it has occurred nor a purely noncognitive awareness that fails to reflect the specific character of the belief and its content. Instead it is an intrinsic and constitutive awareness of the propositional and assertive content of the belief.[8]

Because of its nonapperceptive, constituent character, this "built-in" awareness of content, as it might be described, neither requires any justification itself, nor for that matter even admits of any. Indeed, as far as I can see, such a nonapperceptive, constituent awareness of content is strictly *infallible* in pretty much the way that foundationalist views have traditionally claimed, but which most have long since abandoned. Since it is in virtue of this constitutive or "built-in" awareness of content that the belief is the particular belief that it is with the specific content that it has, rather than some other belief or some other sort of state, there is apparently no way in which this awareness of content could be mistaken—simply because there is no independent fact or situation for it to be mistaken about.

It is by appeal to this intrinsic, constitutive awareness of propositional and assertive content that the metabelief that I have the first-level belief can, I suggest, be justified. Such a constitutive awareness of content seems obviously enough to constitute in and by itself, at least if other things are equal, a reason for thinking that the metabelief that I have an occurrent belief with that very content is true (or, perhaps more realistically, for thinking that a metabelief that gives a less detailed, more abstract description of the first-order content, but one that the actual, more specific content falls under, is true). The point here, elaborated further below, is that the metabelief is a *description* of the very content involved in the constitutive awareness of content, so that by consciously having that constitutive awareness, I am in an ideal position to judge whether or not this description is correct.

In this way, such a metabelief can have precisely the epistemic status required by foundationalism: it can be justified in the sense of there being a clear and internally accessible reason for thinking that it is true, but the reason in question can be such as to avoid any appeal to a further belief that would itself be in need of justification—though we now see that it is the first-level constitutive or "built-in" awareness of content, rather than the metabelief that it justifies, that turns out to be the ultimate source of justification.

The infallibility of the "built-in" awareness does not, of course, extend to the apperceptive metabelief: it would still be possible to apperceptively misapprehend one's own belief, that is, to have a second-level belief that does not accurately reflect the content contained in the constitutive or "built-in" awareness constitutive of the first-level belief. Such a mistake might be a case of mere inattention, or it might result from the complexity or obscurity of the belief content itself or from some further problem. But unless there is some special reason in a particular case to think that the chances of such a misapprehension are large, this possibility of error does not seem to prevent the second-level metabelief from being justifiable by appeal to the first-level constituent awareness. This is just to say that while such justification is defeasible in various ways, it is adequate until and unless it is defeated, rather than requiring an independent and prior showing of reliability.

The foregoing account of the foundational status of metabeliefs about one's own occurrent beliefs or thoughts seems to me to possess a good deal of intuitive plausibility, but this is hardly enough to show that it is correct. The best way to defend it further is to examine and defend the underlying view of the nature of consciousness upon which it rests. This will be the job of the next section.

III. Two Theories of Consciousness

As just suggested, what underlies the foundationalist picture just offered is a view concerning the nature of consciousness itself: the view that a consciousness of the appropriate sort of content is an intrinsic, constitutive feature of a conscious mental state,[9] one that is a part of its own internal character and depends not at all on any further apperceptive state. Perhaps the best way to both clarify and defend this view is to contrast it with the only very clear alternative, a view that has become known as the "higher-order thought" theory of consciousness, first explicitly advanced and defended by David Rosenthal.[10] According to Rosenthal's view, consciousness is not an intrinsic property of any mental state. Instead, one mental state becomes conscious only by being the object of a *second* mental state, a higher-order thought that one is in the first mental state.

The issue between these two views of the nature of consciousness is obviously crucial for the defensibility of the version of foundationalism suggested in the previous section (and elaborated further below). If Rosenthal is right, the conscious dimension of my first-level belief or thought that foundationalism is much more defensible than most philosophers think depends on the existence of an appropriate second-order thought, namely, the thought that I have the occurrent belief that foundationalism is much more defensible than most philosophers think. In consequence (as he never quite says explicitly but seems clearly to intend), there would be no consciousness at all of the content of the first-level belief or thought, were that content not apprehended in a second-order thought. And if this were so, then conscious awareness of the first-level content would apparently occur only as a part of the content of the second-order thought, so that there would be no "built-in" or constitutive awareness of the content of the first-order belief or thought to appeal to for the justification of the metabelief discussed in the previous section. And since such a second-order thought appears to be just as much in need of justification as the original metabelief—indeed it might apparently just be that metabelief in an occurrent form—appealing to its content also yields no foundational justification. Thus if the higher-order thought theory of consciousness is correct, the foundationalist view that I am trying to develop will not work.

Fortunately, however, there is a clear and decisive reason why the higher-order thought theory cannot be correct. (A second, somewhat less decisive but still weighty reason will emerge later.) This arises by first noticing that the higher-order thoughts whose occurrence supposedly confers consciousness on lower-order thoughts cannot themselves all be conscious. One such higher-order thought may of course be conscious by virtue of being the object of a still higher-order thought, but since it is reasonably clear that an infinite hierarchy of such higher-order thoughts does not and probably cannot exist, there must in any sequence of such thoughts, each having the previous one as its object, be a highest-order thought in that sequence that is not in turn the object of a still higher-order thought and thus, according to the higher-order thought theory, that is not itself conscious. All this Rosenthal accepts and indeed seems to advocate, [467] though, if I am right, without fully appreciating its significance.

Now consider again my earlier example of my first-order conscious belief that foundationalism is much more defensible than most philosophers think. On Rosenthal's account, as we have seen, the status of this thought as conscious must result from a second-level thought that I have the first-level thought, rather than from a "built-in" or constitutive conscious awareness. And let us suppose, for the sake of simplicity, that the second-order thought is in this case not itself the object of any higher-order thought, and so, according to his account, is not itself conscious. Rosenthal seems to regard this as the most typical case, [465-66] and considering more complicated possibilities would yield the same ultimate result, albeit in a somewhat more convoluted way.

The problem is now to understand how and why according to this picture I am conscious of the content of my first-level belief or thought at all. I am not conscious of that content merely by virtue of having the first-order thought. And though the first-level content is reflected in the content of the second-level thought, *I am not conscious of that second-level content either*, on Rosenthal's view, since there is no higher-order thought about it. Thus it is entirely obscure where the consciousness of the first-level content is supposed to come from or to reside. If the first-order thought is not in itself conscious and the second-order thought is not in itself conscious, and if there are in this case no higher-order thoughts (which would yield only a longer sequence of nonconscious thoughts), then there seems to be no consciousness of the first-level content present at all—contrary to the initial stipulation that we are dealing with a first-level thought that is (somehow) conscious.

My diagnosis is that Rosenthal (along with many others including, perhaps, Descartes himself) has confused two subtly but crucially different things: first, the consciousness of the *content* of a conscious mental state, which is, I have suggested, intrinsic to the occurrence of that state itself; and, second, the reflective or apperceptive consciousness of that state itself, the consciousness *that* such a state has occurred, which I agree requires a second-level or apperceptive state. This confusion is plainly reflected in Rosenthal's statement that "conscious states are simply mental states we are conscious of being in." [462] Conflating these two things leads quite inevitably to the view that a mental state could be intrinsically conscious only by somehow paradoxically having *both* its ordinary content and the further, self-referential content that it itself occurs. Rosenthal is surely right to reject such a view, [469-70] but wrong that it is the only alternative to his higher-order thought theory.

One important point worth adding here is that if a particular mental state lacks such an intrinsic awareness of its own content (which I have not argued here to be impossible), one may still come in some way to have a higher-order thought that it (the lower-order state) exists. But such a higher-order thought, even if it is itself intrinsically conscious in the way indicated, would not, contrary to Rosenthal's claim, somehow transmute the state that is its object into a conscious state, even though the subject would be conscious *of* that state as an object. An important corollary of this point is that in such a situation, the subject would be conscious of the content of the lower-order state only indirectly and only as described or characterized in the content of the higher-order state—which description may of course be incomplete or less than fully accurate and will in any case be in conceptual terms. Especially where the state in question is a qualitative or sensory state with a content that is not itself conceptual (see further below), there is all the difference in the world between an external and conceptual awareness that it occurs and an actual conscious awareness of the qualitative or sensory content itself.

My conclusion here is that the higher-order thought theory is untenable and indeed obviously so, with the only apparent alternative being the view, advocated above, that an awareness of the appropriate sort of content is an intrinsic, constitutive feature of those mental states that are conscious—thus making it possible, as discussed above, to appeal to that awareness to justify a foundational belief.

IV. Foundational Beliefs about Sensory Experience

If I am right, the foregoing provides at least a sketch of how a certain specific sort of belief, namely, an apperceptive metabelief about an occurrent belief of one's own, can be basic in the sense of there being an internally available reason why it is likely to be true without that reason depending on any further belief or other cognitive state that is itself in need of justification. Apart from possible objections based on externalist theories of belief content, which I find extremely implausible but have no time to go into here,[11] the account in question also seems extremely obvious, too obvious to warrant discussing, were it not that so many, my earlier self included, have managed to miss it.

Where does this leave us? Even this much of a foundationalist ingredient would be a valuable addition to erstwhile coherence theories like my own earlier view.[12] Though there would still be a serious problem of what to say about nonoccurrent beliefs, to which the account sketched so far is not directly applicable, at least a good deal of the problem of access to one's own beliefs would be solved. It is doubtful, however, that foundational beliefs about my own beliefs, even if worries stemming from the occurrent-dispositional distinction are set aside, are enough by themselves to provide an adequate basis for justification of beliefs about the objective physical world.[13] And in any case, having shown how a foundational grasp of the content of one's own beliefs is possible, there is an analogous, albeit somewhat more complicated and problematic possibility with respect to the contents of other kinds of experience, especially sensory or perceptual experience, that needs to be considered.

Consider then a state of, for example, visual experience, such as the one that I am presently having as I look out over this room. Like an occurrent belief, such an experience is a conscious state. What this means, I suggest, is that, in a way that parallels the account of occurrent belief or thought offered above, it automatically involves a constitutive or "built-in," nonapperceptive awareness of its own distinctive sort of content, namely sensory or experiential content.[14] And, again in parallel fashion, such a constitutive awareness of sensory content is in no need of justification and is indeed infallible in the sense that there is no sort of mistake that is even relevant to it. Since it is this awareness of sensory content that gives my experiential state the specific content that it has and thus constitutes it as the specific experiential state that it is, there is no logical room for this awareness to be mistaken about the content in question. And thus such an awareness of sensory content is also apparently available to justify foundational beliefs.

Before we embrace this idea too eagerly, however, there is a recently popular objection that needs to be addressed. This objection, which is present with various degrees of explicitness in the thought of philosophers as different as Popper, Sellars, Davidson, and Rorty,[15] begins with the idea that the distinctive content of a sensory or perceptual experience, that content the awareness of which makes the experience the very experience that it is, is nonpropositional and nonconceptual in character—where what this means is at least that this most basic awareness of sensory content is not couched in general or classificatory terms, is not a propositional awareness that the experience falls under general categories or universals. And from this the conclusion is drawn that such an awareness cannot stand in any intelligible justificatory relation to a belief formulated in propositional and conceptual terms, and hence that the relation between the two must be merely causal. As Davidson puts it:

> The relation between a sensation and a belief cannot be logical, since sensations are not beliefs or other propositional attitudes. What then is the relation? The answer is, I think, obvious: the relation is causal. Sensations cause some beliefs and in *this* sense are the basis or ground of those beliefs. But a causal explanation of a belief does not show how or why the belief is justified.[16]

And if this were correct, what I have been calling the constitutive or "built-in" awareness of sensory content, even though it undeniably exists, would be incapable of playing any justificatory role and thus would apparently have no real epistemological significance.

The premise of this objection, namely the claim that sensory experience is essentially nonconceptual in character, seems to me both true and important. At least part of the point is that the content of, for example, the visual experience that I am having as I look out over this room is far too specific, detailed, and variegated to be adequately captured in any conceptual or propositional formulation—or at least in any that I am presently able to formulate or even understand. Moreover, even if we imagine an ideally complete and fine-grained conceptual description, it seems clear that thinking in conceptual terms of, for example,

very specific shades of color in some complicated pattern is not at all the same
thing as actually experiencing the pattern of colors itself. (Here we see the second objection, alluded to above, to the higher-order thought theory of consciousness: a higher-order conceptual thought could not account for the distinctive sort
of consciousness that a conscious sensory state involves.)

But although I confess to being one of those who has in the past been influenced by this objection, it now seems to me that its conclusion simply does not
follow from its premise. For even if we grant and indeed insist that the specific
content of the experience is itself nonpropositional and nonconceptual, it, like
various other kinds of nonconceptual phenomena, can of course still be conceptually described with various degrees of detail and precision. The relation between
the nonconceptual content and such a conceptual description thereof may not be
logical, as Davidson uses the term, but it is also obviously not merely causal.
Rather it is a *descriptive* relation. And where such a relation of description exists, the character of the nonconceptual object can obviously constitute a kind of
reason or basis for thinking that the description is true or correct (or equally, of
course, untrue or incorrect).

Such a reason is, of course, only available to one who has some sort of independent access to the character of the nonconceptual item, that is, an access that
does not depend on the conceptual description itself. In the most usual sorts of
cases, for example, where it is some physical object or situation that is being
described, one could have an access that is independent of the description in question only by having a second conceptual state embodying a second, perhaps more
specific description, and this second description would of course itself equally
require justification, so that no foundational justification would result. But in the
very special case we are concerned with, where the nonconceptual item being
described is *itself* a conscious state, one can be aware of its character via the constitutive or "built-in" awareness of content without the need for a further conceptual description and thereby be in a position to recognize that a belief about that
state is correct.

Thus where I have a conscious state of sensory experience, I am, as already
argued, aware of the specific sensory content of that state simply by virtue of
having that experience. And thus if an apperceptive belief that I entertain purports to describe or conceptually characterize that perceptual content, albeit no
doubt incompletely, and if I understand the descriptive content of that belief, that
is, understand what an experience would have to be like in order to satisfy the
conceptual description, then I seem to be in a good, indeed an ideal, position to
judge whether the conceptual description is accurate as far as it goes, and if so, to
be thereby justified in accepting the belief. Here again there is no reason to think
that mistake is impossible and thus no reason to think that such an apperceptive
belief is infallible or indubitable. But as long as there is no special reason for
suspecting that a mistake has occurred, the fact that such a belief seems to accurately characterize the conscious experience that it purports to describe seems to
provide an entirely adequate basis for thinking that the description is correct, and
hence an adequate basis for justification.

Here indeed we seem to have exactly the sort of direct comparison or "confrontation" between a conceptual description and the nonconceptual chunk of

reality that it purports to describe which seems intuitively to be essential if our conceptual descriptions are ever to make contact with reality in a verifiable way, but which many philosophers, myself again alas included, have rejected as impossible. Such a confrontation is only possible, to be sure, where the reality in question is itself a conscious state and where the description in question pertains to the conscious content of that very state, but in that very specific case it seems to be entirely unproblematic. Thus we can see that the given is, after all, not a myth!

I am inclined to suspect that it is this sort of nonapperceptive, intrinsic awareness of the content of a conscious state that epistemologists such as those mentioned earlier had at least primarily in mind in their use of the notion of "direct acquaintance" or "immediate awareness." But if this is right, then discussions of direct acquaintance were often needlessly obscure, suggesting as they did some sort of mysteriously authoritative or infallible apprehension of an independent cognitive object, rather than an awareness that is simply constitutive of a conscious state itself. Moreover, the claim of some proponents of direct acquaintance that one might possibly be directly acquainted with physical objects or their surfaces simply makes no sense on the present account of what direct acquaintance really amounts to, thus perhaps vindicating the frequent claim of other proponents of this concept that one can be directly acquainted only with one's own mental states.[17] I also believe that it is this sort of constitutive or "built-in" awareness of the content of a conscious state that Chisholm had in mind in speaking of states that are "self-presenting,"[18] a terminology that seems rather more appropriate to the phenomenon in question than "acquaintance." Alas, he did not succeed in making the idea sufficiently clear to philosophers like myself, though it now seems to me that at the very least a substantial part of the fault lies with those who failed to understand.

The foregoing discussion seems to me to establish that a potential foundation for empirical justification genuinely exists, consisting, more or less as traditional foundationalists thought, of beliefs about the content of sensory experience (and the content of other conscious states). But while such a result is necessary for the defense of a traditional foundationalism, it is obviously very far from sufficient, leaving a host of further questions and issues to be dealt with. In the final two sections, I will try to say a little about some of these, though the largest and most important one of all, namely, the problem of the external world itself, will have to remain largely untouched.

V. The Conceptual Formulation of Sensory Content

Perhaps the most immediate question is what form the allegedly foundational beliefs about sensory content actually take and the related issue of whether it is plausible to suppose that ordinary people actually have any such beliefs.

Here I am assuming that for the content of sensory experience to play any justificatory role, it is necessary that such content be conceptually formulated in beliefs that are explicitly about it. Things would be far easier if it were plausible to hold, as some have,[19] that nonconceptual content could somehow directly justify beliefs that are not directly about it, for example, that are directly about physical objects, without that content needing to be itself formulated in conceptual terms. It seems to me, however, that any such view is untenable, that Davidson and the others are right in thinking that there is no intelligible relation of justification between nonconceptual sensory content and conceptual beliefs in general. I have argued that such a justificatory relation can exist in the specific case where the conceptual belief is a purported description of the conscious experiential content itself, but I think that this is the only sort of case where it makes clear and intelligible sense. Thus it is impossible, in my view, for a foundationalist to avoid the issues of what form such descriptions might actually take and of whether or not we actually have any.

These issues would be relatively simple to deal with if it were plausible to suppose that we are able to conceptually formulate the given content in phenomenological terms that are as close as possible to the apparent character of the given experience itself—in terms of something like the pure sense-datum language or concepts envisaged by various philosophers earlier in this century. The advocates of such views have usually assumed that the resulting description of, for example, visual experience would be in terms of patches of color arranged in a two-dimensional visual space, and I have no desire at present to quarrel with such a picture. The idea that such a purely phenomenological description could accurately capture the content of experience would nowadays be rejected by many as wrong-headed in principle,[20] but this now seems to me to be a mistake. I can see no reason why it would not be possible for us to have the conceptual resources to provide such a phenomenological description of experience to any level of precision and accuracy desired, even though it seems obvious that we would always fall short of an ideally complete description.

But even if an account of experience in phenomenological terms represents a theoretical possibility, the idea that our main conceptual grasp of the content of experience is in such terms faces two obvious difficulties of a more narrowly practical sort. First, we clearly do not in fact possess the needed conceptual resources, even if I am right that it would be possible in principle to possess them. It is important, however, not to exaggerate this point. Most people are capable of giving reasonably precise and accurate phenomenological or at least quasi-phenomenological descriptions of some aspects of their experience, and a person, such as an artist or a wine taster, who cultivates this ability can often do a good deal better. But it is doubtful whether even those whose abilities of this sort are the best developed are in a position to conceptually formulate a strictly phenomenological characterization of sense experience that is sufficiently detailed and precise to capture all or even most of its justificatory significance for claims about the physical world (assuming for the moment that it has such significance). And in any case, it is exceedingly clear that most of us do not even begin to approach such a capacity. Second, even if we did possess the needed conceptual resources, it seems abundantly clear that the time and effort required to formulate justificatorily adequate descriptions of experience in such terms, whether overtly in language or internally to oneself, would be prohibitive from a practical standpoint.

But if our conceptual formulations of the given content of sensory experience are not, at least for the most part, couched in purely phenomenological terms, the only very obvious alternative is that we conceptually grasp such content in terms of the physical objects and situations that we would be inclined on the basis of that experience, other things being equal, to think we are perceiving. Thus, for example, my primary conceptual grasp of my present visual experience characterizes it as the sort of experience that in the absence of countervailing considerations would lead me to think that I am perceiving a moderately large room of a specifiable shape, containing many chairs, a variety of people, and so forth, all of which could be spelled out at great length. The usual way of putting this is to say that what I am conceptually aware of is certain physical-object *appearances* or apparent physical objects—or, in a slightly more technical terminology, of ways of being "appeared to."[21] Where the appearance in question is a visual appearance, we may say instead that it *looks* as though there are objects of the sorts indicated, and analogously for other sensory modalities.[22]

Many philosophers have questioned whether ordinary people in ordinary perceptual situations normally or standardly have beliefs about the nonconceptual content of their sensory experience, even ones that are couched in such appearance terms. I am not convinced that this issue has the importance that is often ascribed to it, because it does not seem to me in any clear way to be a requirement for an adequate philosophical account of empirical justification that ordinary beliefs will turn out to be fully and explicitly justified. But it nonetheless seems to me that an ordinary person who has, for example, a visual belief about a certain sort of physical object plausibly has something that is tantamount to a grasp of the character of his visual experience in physical-object appearance terms: such a person is after all surely aware that the perceptual claim in question is a result of vision, that is, that he sees the object; and this seems to amount to at least an implicit realization that his or her visual experience is such as to make it look as though an object of that sort is there. That an ordinary person would not couch matters in such explicitly philosophical terms must, of course, be granted, but this does not seem to me to show that they are not aware of what the philosophical account more explicitly formulates.

But while this seems to me to be the main answer to the question of how we grasp sensory content in conceptual terms, the potential for misunderstanding its significance is very serious, and many philosophers seem to me to have succumbed to this danger. In particular, it is crucially important to distinguish a description of experience that merely indicates what sort of physical objects and situations seem or appear, on the basis of that experience, to be present from one that embodies some further causal or relational claim about the connection between experience and the physical realm, one whose justification would clearly have to appeal to something beyond the experienced content itself.

A useful example of the sort of danger that I am warning against is provided by Susan Haack in her recent book on epistemology, in the course of which she attempts to give a specification of the evidential force of a state of perceptual experience. Her suggestion is that this can be captured by a set of propositions ascribing the perceptual states to the subject in question. Thus, for example, such an ascription might say that the subject "is in the sort of perceptual state a person would be in, in normal circumstances, when looking at a rabbit three feet

away and in good light" or "is in the sort of perceptual state a normal subject
would be in, in normal circumstances, when getting a brief glimpse of a fast-
moving rabbit at dusk."[23] Haack's discussion of this point is perhaps not as
clear or full as one might like, but the specific formulations offered make it reasonable to suppose that these characterizations are intended to describe the experience in terms of the physical situations that are *causally* or *lawfully* connected
with it, rather than in terms of its intrinsic content. This, however, is precisely
the sort of description that *cannot* be justified by appeal to the experienced content alone. My experience may be such as to incline me to think that a rabbit is
present, but the experience cannot by itself reveal that it is actually of the sort
that is normally caused by rabbits. A useful way of putting the point is to say
that the claims about physical appearances or ways of being appeared to that
constitute our primary conceptual formulations of sensory experience must be
understood in something like what Chisholm has called the "descriptive, non-
comparative" sense of the terms or concepts in question,[24] for only in that sense
can the claim to be "appeared to" in a certain way be adequately justified simply
by appeal to our constitutive, nonconceptual awareness of sensory content.

As already argued, it seems quite obvious that we have the ability to grasp or
represent the character of our perceptual experience fairly accurately, albeit
somewhat obliquely, in terms of such physical object appearances. But once
illegitimate construals like Haack's are set aside, it is far from obvious exactly
what such characterizations of experience really amount to. In giving them, we
seem to be relying on a tacitly grasped and, we think, mutually understood correlation or association, perhaps learned or perhaps at least partially innate, between
experiential features and the physical situations of which they are taken to be
appearances, one that we are confidently guided by in the vast majority of cases,
even though we are unable even to begin to formulate it explicitly.

To speak here of a "correlation" might suggest the idea that it is a mere correlation, that the experiential content and the corresponding propositional claim
about physical objects are only externally coordinated, without being connected
with each other in any more intimate way. This, however, is not the view that I
mean to be advocating. On the contrary, as discussed a bit further in the final
section, it seems intuitively pretty clear that the experiential content is in itself
somehow strongly suggestive of or in some interesting way isomorphic to the
correlated physical situation. But however this correlation ultimately works, the
important issue is whether the beliefs about the physical world that we adopt on
the basis of it are at least likely to be true, something that cannot be simply
assumed.

VI. The Problem of the External World

This brings me then, finally and necessarily briefly, to the most important issue
that arises for this sort of position: If the foregoing is at least approximately the
right way to understand our primary conceptual representations of the given content of sensory experience, how, if at all, do such representations contribute to
the justification of beliefs about the physical world? In particular, how does the

fact that my given sensory experience can be correctly described, in light of the tacit correlation just mentioned, as the appearance of a certain sort of physical object or situation contribute to the *justification* of the claim that such an object or situation is actually present and being perceived? This is of course the ultimate question in this general area, one that would take far more time than is available here to deal with adequately. For the moment, I will therefore have to be content with a brief canvassing of what I take to be the main alternative possibilities for a nonskeptical solution.

First. Perhaps the most historically standard solution is the reductive phenomenalist attempt to define physical object concepts in terms of sensory appearance concepts, thereby making the connection between claims about sensory appearances and claims about physical objects a matter of conceptual or analytic necessity. Though there are difficult issues of conceptual priority involved,[25] it seems to me that this approach is likely to succeed for the specific case of secondary qualities like color. But the problems afflicting a more global phenomenalist approach are both well known and, in my judgment, clearly fatal.

Second. A quite different solution is advocated by H. H. Price[26] and, in what seems to be a rather seriously qualified form, by Chisholm. The core idea of this view is that the mere occurrence of a physical appearance or state of being appeared to confers prima facie justification on the corresponding physical claim. Chisholm's own version of this solution, presented in the most recent edition of *Theory of Knowledge*,[27] appeals to a logical relation of "tending to make evident" that is alleged to exist between claims or beliefs about sensory appearances and the corresponding claims or beliefs about the actual perception of physical objects. Thus my belief that my present visual experience involves appearances of a distinctive group of people in a distinctive room, or my belief that I am being appeared to in the corresponding ways, *tends to make evident* my belief that I am perceiving such people and such a room and that they really exist in the physical world. Such a tendency is capable of being defeated by countervailing evidence, but where no such defeater is present, the claim of genuine perception is justified.

My difficulty with this sort of view is that it seems to me very implausible to suppose that such a logical relation of "tending to make evident" or "tending to justify" genuinely exists between an individual belief about physical appearances and the corresponding belief about physical reality. To be sure, Chisholm's claim is not that any such relation is discernible a priori in itself, but only that it is an a priori consequence of the "general presupposition" or "faith," roughly, that epistemological success is possible.[28] The skeptical implications of ascribing no stronger epistemic status than that to the claim that such a connection between appearances and physical reality really exists seem pretty serious in themselves. But over and above that, my objection is that if the belief about appearance is construed, as I have argued that it must be construed, as merely a useful though oblique way of describing the nonconceptual content of sensory experience, then there is no apparent way that it could by itself have any direct or immediate bearing of this sort on the truth or likely truth of the corresponding physical claim, assuming that claim to be nonreductively understood—and thus no way that there could be any such logical relation of "tending to make evident" or "tending to justify," whether a priori knowable or not.

One way to argue this point is to notice that if descriptions of the given content of experience in terms of physical object appearances are understood in the way just indicated, rather than as embodying some further claim or inference for which additional justification would be required, then it would be a mistake to think that they have any epistemological, as opposed to practical, advantage over descriptions of such experience in purely phenomenological terms. The experiential content being described is the same in either case, and its justificatory capacity is not somehow enhanced by failing to conceptualize it in the terms that would be most explicitly descriptive of it. But there seems to me to be no plausibility at all to the idea that a purely phenomenological description of the same experience that is in fact conceptualized as a particular physical object appearance (or state of being appeared to) would by itself have any tendency to justify or render evident the corresponding claim about the physical world. At the very least, some more specific account would have to be given of why this is supposed to be so.

Third. My own fairly tentative suggestion would be that the basis for the needed inference from sensory appearance to physical reality is to be found in several fundamental facts about such appearances. Two of these were noticed by Locke and Berkeley, among others: first, the involuntary, spontaneous character of such appearances; and second, the fact that they fit together and reinforce each other in, dare I say, a *coherent* fashion, presenting a relatively seamless and immensely complicated (albeit also incomplete) picture of an ongoing world.[29] These two fundamental facts are, of course, the central ones appealed to by Locke in justifying his inference from sensory ideas to the external world; and by Berkeley, in justifying his inference to the God who is supposed to produce our ideas. In both cases, the underlying idea, rather more explicit in Berkeley, is that some *explanation* is needed for the combination of involuntariness and coherence, and that the conclusion advocated by the philosopher in question is thereby justified as the best explanation of the facts in question.[30]

I once believed that an inference on something like this basis, to Locke's conclusion rather than Berkeley's, was ultimately cogent, but this now seems to me mistaken. No doubt the combination of spontaneity and intricate coherence requires *some* explanation, which is just to say that it is unlikely to result from chance. But why an explanation in physical object terms, rather than any of the other possibilities (including Berkeley's) that so obviously exist? What makes the physical explanation so obviously salient is our ingrained inclination to describe the experiential content in physical terms (or, indeed, to leap directly to a physical claim with no explicit acknowledgment of the experiential premise). Since it is, however, this very correlation between experience and physical object claims whose justification is at issue, no appeal to that correlation can as such have any justificatory weight.

The obvious response at this point would appeal to the idea, briefly mentioned earlier, that the correlation between experiential content and physical objects is not a mere correlation, that is, that there are features of the experiential content itself that are strongly and systematically isomorphic or structurally similar to the correlated physical situations. It is only if something like this is so that there could be any reason to prefer the physical explanation of experience to the various others that might be given. I have already suggested that such a view seems to me intuitively plausible, and I think (perhaps somewhat optimistically) that it is ultimately correct. But an account of how this isomorphism and the inference to the physical world that, I have suggested, must be based on it would go in detail is a long story that I have neither the space here nor very likely, at present, the ability to recount.

Notes

1. For a much fuller discussion of coherentism and its problems, along with an earlier sketch of the foundationalist view presented here, see BonJour (forthcoming, a).

2. There are, of course, versions of empirical foundationalism that hold that at least some perceptual beliefs about physical objects are themselves basic or foundational. See, for example, Quinton (1973). My reasons for rejecting such views can be gleaned from the account of foundational beliefs offered below.

3. I will assume here without further discussion that an adequate reason for thinking that an empirical belief is true could not consist entirely of beliefs that are justified a priori.

4. For a defense of this conception of self-evidence in relation to a priori justification, see BonJour (1997).

5. See Lewis (1943) and Fumerton (1995).

6. In BonJour (1985): Chapter 4.

7. The original source of the dilemma is Wilfrid Sellars. See Sellars (1963), pp. 127-96, esp. pp. 131-32, and (1975), pp. 295-347. For my own previous development and elaboration of it, see BonJour (1985): Chapter 4.

8. I interpret this as "going between the horns of the dilemma," because I am construing the horns as embodying the development and elaboration indicated in the earlier discussion and just summarized in the text, according to which the conceptual horn involves a conceptual or propositional awareness that a state of the specified sort occurs. Though the constitutive awareness of the content of the belief of course involves the concepts that figure in that content, it is not a conceptual or propositional awareness *that* I have a belief with the content in question, and so, as explained further in the text, does not raise any issue of justification. But one could instead interpret the present argument as showing that the conceptual side of the conceptual/nonconceptual dichotomy is not necessarily incompatible with foundationalism after all, because it need not involve such a propositional awareness; this would amount to "grasping one of the horns of the dilemma" rather than going between them. (On this latter interpretation, the analogous possibility for sensory experience, discussed below, would show that the nonconceptual horn also includes a possibility that is compatible with foundationalism.) I am grateful to Matthias Steup for helping me to see this alternative way of viewing the relation of the constitutive awareness of content to the Sellarsian dilemma.

9. Though not necessarily of all mental states—that is a further issue.

10. Rosenthal (1989), reprinted (1991). Page references in the text are to this reprint.

11. For some relevant discussion, see BonJour (1991).

12. In BonJour (1985).

13. Some of the problems with coherentism discussed in the paper cited in note 1 are also relevant to this point.

14. Such content is not, as we will see, propositional or conceptual in character, and this may seem to some to make the very word "content" inappropriate. But while agreeing that there is a certain potential for confusion here, I know of no better term for what one is conscious of in having sensory or phenomenal states of consciousness, and so will continue to employ it, with the warning that the two sorts of content are importantly different and should not be conflated.

15. See Popper (1959): §§ 25-30; Sellars (1963); Davidson (1983); and Rorty (1979): Chapters 3 and 4. (As will be obvious, this objection is not unrelated to the Sellarsian dilemma discussed above, though still different enough in its explicit formulation to warrant separate treatment.)

16. Davidson (1983): 428.

17. I am limiting my attention here to claims of direct acquaintance with matters of concrete and contingent fact. The application of the idea of direct acquaintance to necessary truths and abstract entities generally raises issues that lie beyond the scope of the present paper.

18. See, for example, Chisholm (1989): 18-19.

19. See, for example, Moser (1989). Moser's view is that nonconceptual contents justify physical object claims in virtue of the fact that the latter explain the former, but he says almost nothing about how the explanatory relation in question is supposed to work.

20. See, for example, Strawson (1979).

21. As this last formulation suggests, I am inclined to favor an "adverbial" construal of sensory experience, as opposed to the "act-object" construal advocated by the sense-datum theory. But the ontological issue that separates these two sorts of views does not, in my judgment, make any difference at all to the epistemological issues that are the focus of the present paper.

22. Many philosophers have objected to the idea that, for example, ordinary "looks" statements can be construed as descriptions of nonconceptual sensory content. See, for example, Sellars (1963): §§ 10-23. I do not have space to enter into this controversy here and must content myself with saying that the objections in question seem to me to show at most that there are other senses of "looks" besides the one that I want here (e.g., one that indicates a tentative or guarded opinion about what is actually there), but they have no serious tendency to show that the sense presently at issue does not exist. For further discussion of this issue, see Jackson (1977): Chapter 2.

23. Haack (1993): 80.

24. See, for example, Chisholm (1989): 23.

25. See, for example, the discussion of this issue in the first of Sellars' Carus lectures (1981).

26. See Price (1950): Chapter 7.

27. Chisholm (1989): 46-54, 64-68, 71-74.

28. Chisholm (1989): 4-6, 72-73.

29. See Locke (1975): Book IV, Chapter xi, and Berkeley (1965): §§ 28-30.

30. For a useful discussion and elaboration of Locke's argument, see Mackie (1976): Chapter 2. See also BonJour (1985): Chapter 8, for some of the ideas that I take to be relevant, even though they are couched there in terms of a coherence theory.

Part II

Comments

Chapter 3

Nondoxastic Foundationalism

John L. Pollock

I. Introduction

Fumerton and BonJour have presented two very interesting theories. They are also strikingly similar in some important ways. I think we can learn a lot about epistemology and perceptual knowledge by considering those theories carefully. Let me begin by making some distinctions and laying some groundwork.

Both Fumerton and BonJour call their theories "foundations theories," although I am not sure that, by certain standards, they really are. This, in itself, is just a matter of terminology, but it is good to make the terminology precise in order to avoid conflating different views. Foundations theories are so-called because they propose that our knowledge is rooted in foundations provided by perception, broadly conceived. Schematically, we can picture foundations theories as trees of beliefs sprouting above a somehow secure foundation, with beliefs constituting the nodes of the tree and the branches representing some kind of support, standardly conceived as the result of reasoning. The theories of Fumerton and BonJour both have this structure. However, not all theories having this structure have always been called "foundations theories."

I constructed a taxonomy of epistemological theories in my book *Contemporary Theories of Knowledge* (1987), and some of the distinctions made there are germane to understanding what kinds of theories are being proposed by Fumerton and BonJour. In particular, I defined *doxastic theories* to be theories that endorse the *doxastic assumption*, according to which the justification, or justifiability, of an epistemic agent's beliefs is determined exclusively by what beliefs the agent holds. There is a simple argument for the doxastic assumption, which many philosophers have found convincing—in deciding what to believe, it is impossible for us to take account of any consideration except insofar as we have a belief about it, so we cannot appeal to anything other than our beliefs, and they alone can be relevant in determining whether our epistemic decision is a rational one.

In dividing up the epistemological turf, I took foundations theories and coherence theories to partition the class of doxastic theories. Foundations theories are doxastic theories according to which there is a privileged subclass of beliefs that do not stand in need of independent justification and provide the foundation for justifying any other beliefs. Coherence theories are any doxastic theories that are not foundations theories, that is, those in which all beliefs are epistemically on a par with each other in determining what beliefs are justified.

So defined, foundations theories possess the kind of foundational structure typically associated with them. However, there can be other theories possessing such a foundational structure as well that are not foundations theories. These would be theories that deny the doxastic assumption, taking the foundation to be something other than beliefs. In *Contemporary Theories of Knowledge*,[1] I defended one such theory, which I called *direct realism*. According to this theory, epistemic justification has a foundational structure, but the foundations consist of our percepts themselves rather than beliefs about our percepts. On this account, something's looking red to me can justify me in thinking that it is red, without the justification passing through a *belief* to the effect that it looks red.

I must acknowledge that the term "direct realism" is not very perspicuous in indicating the content of the theory. It would be clearer to redefine the terminology, distinguishing between "doxastic" and "nondoxastic" foundations theories. Then foundations theories would no longer have to be doxastic theories. For the duration of this paper I will employ this revised terminology. One thing that I want to consider carefully is whether the theories of Fumerton and BonJour are doxastic theories or nondoxastic theories.

II. Arguments Against Doxastic Foundationalism

But before taking up that question, let me lay some more groundwork. First, I gave two general arguments against doxastic foundationalism, and it will be useful to briefly rehearse them here.

The Epistemological Status of Appearance Beliefs

The first argument questions whether beliefs about percepts have the kind of secure epistemic status required for them to provide a foundation. By definition, foundational beliefs can be held justifiably without our having an independent reason for believing them. This is captured by the concept of a prima facie justified belief:

(D1)   A belief is *prima facie justified* for a person S if and only if it is only possible for S to hold the belief unjustifiedly if he has reason for thinking he should not hold the belief (equivalently, it is necessarily true that if S holds the belief and has no reason for thinking he should not then he is justified in holding the belief).

Foundational beliefs must be at least prima facie justified. Foundationalists have generally thought they had an even stronger status, being either *incorrigibly justified* or *incorrigible*:

(D2)   A belief is *incorrigibly justified* for a person S if and only if it is impossible for S to hold the belief but be unjustified in doing so.

(D3)   A proposition P is *incorrigible* for a person S if and only if (1) it is neces-
       sarily true that if S believes P then P is true, and (2) it is necessarily true
       that if S believes ~P then P is false.

(Incorrigibility is defined this way to get around the problem of necessary beliefs—if incorrigibility required only the first condition, then beliefs in necessary
truths would automatically be incorrigible, but we do not always regard such
beliefs as justified.)
    I doubt that beliefs about how things look to us have any of these statuses.
To this effect, I gave the following counterexample in *Contemporary Theories of
Knowledge*. Because shadows on white surfaces are normally gray, most people
think that shadows on snow are gray. But a discovery made fairly early by every
landscape painter is that they are actually blue. A person having the general belief that shadows on snow are gray may, when queried about how a particular
snow-shadow looks to him, reply that it looks gray, without paying any serious
attention to his percept. His belief about how it looks is based upon his general
belief rather than inspection of his percept, and is accordingly wrong. This
shows that the belief is not incorrigible. Furthermore, should his general belief
itself be unjustified, then his belief about how the shadow looks will also be
unjustified, establishing that it is neither incorrigibly justified nor prima facie
justified. This seems to show that beliefs about how things look to us do not
have the logical properties minimally required to serve as foundational beliefs.
    There is a response to this counterexample that has considerable intuitive
pull, at least initially. This is to agree that not all beliefs about how things appear to us are prima facie justified, but those *based upon actually being appeared
to in that way* are. Taken literally, this makes no sense. As I defined it, prima
facie justification is a logical property of propositions. A proposition cannot
have such a property at one time and fail to have it at another. But the claim
actually being made here is presumably a different one, namely, that when we are
appeared to in a certain way, that in and of itself can make us at least defeasibly
justified in believing that we are appeared to in that way. This claim is strikingly similar to some things Fumerton and BonJour have said, and I think it
may well be true. But notice that a theory providing such a foundation for epistemic justification is no longer a doxastic theory. The justifiedness of beliefs is
no longer determined exclusively by *what* we believe. What percepts we have is
also relevant.

Are There Enough Appearance Beliefs?

My second general argument against doxastic foundationalism has a simple
structure. If all of our justified beliefs are inferred in some way from beliefs
about percepts, then we must have *enough* beliefs about percepts to make that
possible. Unfortunately, it does not seem that we do. People rarely have any
beliefs at all about how things look to them. When I look around the room, I
form all sorts of beliefs about physical objects, people, and so on, but I rarely
have any thoughts at all about how things look to me. Of course, I can quite
easily acquire such beliefs by turning my attention inwards, but that requires a

deliberate change of attention and is not something that we ordinarily do when perceiving the world around us. In normal cases of perceptual knowledge, it seems we move directly from our percepts to our beliefs about the world, without going through intermediary beliefs about how things appear to us. This is to endorse a kind of nondoxastic foundationalism rather than a doxastic foundationalism.

Reconsidering the Doxastic Assumption

The preceding considerations seem to favor nondoxastic foundationalism, but there is also an argument against nondoxastic foundationalism that many philosophers have found persuasive, and it is repeated by both Fumerton and BonJour. This argument takes as its premise that in order for a mental state to provide us with a reason for holding a belief, the state must have propositional content, that is, it must be an intentional state. Percepts do not have propositional content. Percepts simply occur to us, and it is only by *inspecting* the percept that we get ourselves into an intentional state of the sort that can provide a reason. The result of inspecting the percept is most naturally regarded as a belief, but we might be moved instead to say that it is an acquaintance or an awareness, thus moving in the direction of Fumerton and BonJour.

Why should we accept the premise of this argument, according to which having a reason for a belief must consist of being in an intentional state? This is intimately connected with the argument I gave earlier for the doxastic assumption. The argument is that in deciding what to believe, we can only take account of something insofar as we have a belief about it, so only beliefs are relevant. It is not hard to see that there is something wrong with this argument. If it were right, we could only take account of our beliefs insofar as we have beliefs about our beliefs, and then an infinite regress would loom. There has to be something about beliefs that makes them the sort of thing we can take account of without having beliefs about them. What could this be?

What is it to take account of something in the course of cognition? It is to use it in our cognitive deliberations. We can take account of anything by having a belief about it, but cognition has to start somewhere, with things that we do not have beliefs about. Obviously, it can start with beliefs. The reason it can start with beliefs is that they are internal states, and cognition is an internal process that can access internal states directly. Cognition works by accessing our beliefs, noting that we have certain beliefs, and using that to trigger the formation of further beliefs. However, it is *cognition* that must note that we have certain beliefs—*we* do not have to note it ourselves. The sense in which cognition notes it is metaphorical—it is the same as the sense in which a computer program accessing a database might be described as noting that some particular item is contained in it.

Epistemologists have a lamentable tendency to over-intellectualize cognition. Human beings are, in some sense, *cognitive machines*. We are unusual machines in that our machinery can turn upon itself and enable us to direct many of our own internal operations. Many of these operations, like reasoning, can proceed mechanically, without any deliberate direction or intervention from us, but when we want to we can directly affect their course. For example, we can, at least to some extent, decide what to think about, decide not to pursue a certain line of investigation, and to pursue another one instead. There must, however, be a limit to the extent to which we are *required* to do this. After all, the processes by which we do it are a subspecies of the very processes in which we are intervening. If we had to explicitly direct all of our cognitive processes, we would also have to direct the ones involved in doing the directing, and we would again have an infinite regress.

The significance of this is that we do not *have* to think about our reasoning in order to reason. It is important, for various reasons, that we *can* think about it when the need arises, but we do not have to and do not usually do it. Thus reasoning can proceed by moving from beliefs to beliefs without our thinking about either reasoning or the beliefs. By virtue of doing the reasoning we are thinking about whatever the beliefs are about, not about the beliefs themselves. This explains the sense in which cognition can take account of our having certain beliefs without our having to have beliefs to the effect that we have those beliefs. But note that it explains much more. In precisely the same sense, cognition can take account of other internal states, for example, percepts, without our having to have beliefs to the effect that we are in those states. Thus there is no reason, in principle, why cognition cannot move directly from percepts to beliefs about the physical objects putatively represented by the percepts.

Procedural Epistemic Justification

One might be tempted to respond that this is all true for cognition, but it does not show anything about epistemic justification—it is quite true that cognition can move directly from percepts to beliefs about physical objects, but when it does those beliefs are not justified. Why would one think that that is true? Only, I think, because they are over-intellectualizing cognition. The thought seems to be that if we are not directly monitoring and directing our cognition, it does not produce justified beliefs. But does that mean that we must also be monitoring and directing our monitoring and directing? If not, why not?

Epistemic justification is a normative notion. It pertains to how we should or should not cognize. There is a temptation to use ethical normativity as our model for normativity. In ethics, we only apply normative assessment to things we do deliberately. We take it as an excuse if an action results from a mechanical process over which the actor has no control, so that he could not have done otherwise. Similarly, one may suppose that the concept of epistemic justification is simply inapplicable to beliefs formed on the basis of cognitive processes not directed in a deliberate way by the cognizer.

The problem with this view is that it would remove almost all of our beliefs from the domain of cognitive assessment, because most of our beliefs are produced by mechanical cognitive processes that we *can* direct to varying degrees but generally do not. This would certainly have the consequence that most of the beliefs that we regard as knowledge would be beyond epistemic assessment. It is perhaps worth noting that if we were designing and building a cognitive agent, it would be crazy to build in too much self-monitoring. You do not want the agent to spend all its time thinking about thinking, so that it never gets around to thinking about the world.

The lesson to be learned from this is that epistemic normativity is not too much like moral normativity. So what is epistemic justification all about? Here we have to be careful. Ten or fifteen years ago epistemologists assumed uncritically that there is just one concept of epistemic justification and all epistemologists are talking about it. That now seems dubious. It has become increasingly apparent in the last ten years that there is more than one important concept that might reasonably be called "epistemic justification," and it seems clear that these different concepts have often been confused with one another in the epistemological literature. The literature on the Gettier problem has highlighted one concept, dear to the hearts of many epistemologists, which is something like "what turns true belief into knowledge." The reliabilist literature, for example, might best be read as pertaining to some such concept as this. But there is at least one other important concept that pertains to "the directing of one's own cognition." This is an essentially first-person concept. In my book *Contemporary Theories of Knowledge*, I proposed that this concept could be understood as descriptive of our procedural knowledge for "how to cognize." That part of epistemology that is more concerned with the procedural aspects of rationality than with the analysis of "S knows that P" can, I urged, be viewed as pursuing a competence theory of cognition, in the same way that theories of grammar in Linguistics are competence theories of language. On this view, the normative language employed in the formulation of both theories of grammar and epistemological theories is a reflection, in part, of the competence/performance distinction that can be drawn in connection with any procedural knowledge.

This view of epistemic justification arises from reflection on the way in which philosophers have traditionally tried to answer questions about how, with epistemic propriety, to perform various cognitive tasks (e.g., reasoning inductively). The standard philosophical methodology has been to propose general principles, like the Nicod principle, or principles of Bayesian inference, or the hypothetico-deductive method, and test them by seeing how they apply to concrete examples. In order to test a principle by applying it to concrete examples, we must know how the example should come out. Thus, for example, Nelson Goodman conclusively refuted a version of the Nicod Principle by contriving his famous "grue/bleen" example.[2] The refutation was conclusive because everyone who looks at the example agrees that it would not be epistemically reasonable to accept the conclusions drawn in accordance with the Nicod Principle. But how do people know that? The standard answer is "philosophical intuition," but that is not much of answer. What is philosophical intuition?

Considerable light can be thrown upon this methodology by comparing it with the methodology employed by linguists studying grammaticality. Linguists try to construct general theories of grammar that will suffice to pick out all and only grammatical sentences. They do this by proposing theories and testing them against particular examples. It is a fact that proficient speakers of a language are able to make grammaticality judgments, judging that some utterances are grammatical and others are not. These grammaticality judgments provide the data for testing theories of grammaticality. It is equally undeniable that human cognizers are able to make judgments about whether, in specified circumstances, particular cognitive acts are rational or irrational. These rationality judgments provide the data for testing theories of rationality.

I can imagine a philosopher arguing that epistemic justification has to do with concepts and logic, so our intuitions about epistemic justification must be a kind of platonic intuition of universals. But no one would be tempted to say the same thing about our intuitions of grammaticality. After all, the details of our language are determined by linguistic convention. Our language could have been different than it is, and if it were, our grammatical intuitions would have been different too.

When we learn a language, we learn *how to do* various things. Knowledge of how to do something is procedural knowledge. For most tasks, there is more than one way to do them. Accordingly, we can learn to do them in different ways, and so have different procedural knowledge. But a general characteristic of procedural knowledge seems to be that once we have it, we can also judge more or less reliably whether we are conforming to it in particular cases. For example, once I have learned how to ride a bicycle, if I lean too far to one side (and thus put myself in danger of falling), I do not have to wait until I fall down to know that I am doing it wrong. I can detect my divergence from what I have learned and attempt to correct it before I fall. Similarly, it is very common for competent speakers of a language to make ungrammatical utterances. But if they reflect upon those utterances, they have the ability to recognize them as ungrammatical and correct them. I suggest that exactly the same thing is true of cognition. We have procedural knowledge for how to cognize, and that carries with it the ability to recognize divergences from that procedural knowledge. That is what our so-called "philosophical intuition" amounts to, at least in the theory of epistemic justification.

Noam Chomsky (1957) introduced the competence/performance distinction. Performance theories are theories about how people in fact behave. A performance theory of language would include, for example, an account of what utterances people actually make under various circumstances, be they grammatical or not. A competence theory, on the other hand, attempts to articulate people's procedural knowledge for how to do various things. A competence theory of language would include a theory of the grammatical rules that people have learned to use in constructing their utterances. Because people do not always conform to their own procedural knowledge, competence and performance can diverge dramatically.

My proposal is that the theories of epistemic justification that philosophers construct by appealing to their intuitions about epistemic propriety are best viewed as competence theories of epistemic cognition. That is, they are attempts to articulate the rules comprising our procedural knowledge for how to cognize. We have no direct access to those rules themselves, but because we can detect (with fair reliability) divergences from our procedural knowledge, we can tell in real or imagined cases whether it would be reasonable to draw various conclusions (i.e., whether doing so would conform to our procedural knowledge). We can use such knowledge about particular cases to confirm general principles about the content of our procedural knowledge.

Unlike linguistic knowledge, it seems pretty clear that large parts of our procedural knowledge of how to cognize are built into us rather than learned. This may be required as a matter of logic—it may prove impossible to get started in learning how to cognize unless we already know how to cognize to some extent. But even if that is not true, it is overwhelmingly likely that evolution has built into us knowledge of how to cognize so that we do not come into the world so epistemically vulnerable as we would otherwise be. This way, we at least know how to get started in learning about the world. This is rather strongly confirmed by the overwhelming agreement untutored individuals exhibit in their procedural knowledge of how to cognize.[3] For example, psychological evidence indicates that everyone finds reasoning with modus ponens to be natural and reasoning with modus tollens to be initially unnatural. (See Wason 1966, and Cheng and Holyoak 1985.) It is unlikely that this is something we have learned. Once we start supplementing our built-in procedural knowledge with learned principles, we are quick to embrace modus tollens as well.

Notice that the rules comprising our procedural knowledge of how to cognize cannot be viewed as mere generalizations about how we do cognize. That would make them descriptions of cognitive performance rather than cognitive competence. Instead, they are the rules that we, in some sense, "try" to conform to. They are the rules perceived divergence from which leads us to correct our cognitive performance to bring it into conformance.

My proposal then is that *epistemic norms* are articulations of our built-in procedural knowledge of how to cognize. A belief is justified in the procedural sense of epistemic justification just in case the cognition giving rise to it conforms to those norms.

It is a standard, and desirable, feature of cognition that beliefs are formed in response to being in various states and without our consciously monitoring the fact that we are in those states. So beliefs formed on that basis can be perfectly well justified. The conclusion I want to draw from this is that nondoxastic foundationalism is an accurate description of certain aspects of our procedural knowledge of how to cognize, and that makes it a true epistemological theory.

Now let me turn to Fumerton and BonJour and discuss their theories in light of the preceding remarks.

III. Fumerton

Fumerton begins by defining a foundationalist to be "someone who claims that there are noninferentially justified beliefs and that all justified beliefs owe their justification ultimately, in part, to the existence of noninferentially justified beliefs."[4] Note that he is not endorsing the doxastic assumption here, because of the "in part." He acknowledges this by noting that Goldman's original version of reliabilism might be a foundationalist theory on this definition.

Fumerton wants *classical* foundationalism to impose a further condition on foundationalism that rules out theories like Goldman's and Nozick's. Fumerton's proposal is that classical foundationalism adds internalism, but he laments that it is quite difficult to say precisely what internalism is. Fumerton has discussed various ways of trying to formulate internalism. One version that he mentions but rejects is *strong access internalism*, which is much like the view discussed above according to which, for justified belief, we must monitor and deliberately direct our cognition.

Noninferentially Justified Belief

Fumerton's main concern in this paper is how to understand the concept of non-inferentially justified belief. He writes, "it has always seemed strange to me to search for foundations in mere *belief*." [11] This seems to constitute a rejection of the doxastic assumption. So Fumerton wants to construct and defend a non-doxastic foundationalism.

To clear the decks for his own theory, Fumerton first adduces considerations intended to undermine the kind of nondoxastic foundationalism I have defended. He writes,

> When you believe I am in pain, my pain does not justify you in believing that I am in pain, so there must be something different about my *relationship* to my pain that enters into the account of what constitutes the justification. It is the fact that I have a kind of *access* to my pain that you do not have that makes my belief noninferentially justified while you must rely on inference. [11]

I agree with these observations. In fact, I have given an explanation for them. My pain is an internal state of me, so it is the kind of thing to which my cognitive processes can have nondoxastic access. Where I want to part company with Fumerton is when, citing BonJour, he takes these observations to support the rejection of the view that what justifies one in believing one is in pain is the pain itself. Why should we think that these observations support that conclusion? On the contrary, it would seem that cognition naturally moves from the pain to the belief that one is in pain. The pain thus procedurally justifies the belief that one is in pain.

Acquaintance

Fumerton's theory is driven by his taking seriously what we might call the *Sellarsian Dilemma*:

> If the foundations consist of intentional states—states with propositional contents—then they stand in need of justification just as much as the belief they support. If the foundations consist of nonintentional states, then there is no way they can justify beliefs.

Because he accepts the first horn of the dilemma, Fumerton seeks a kind of non-intentional state that can justify belief. He proposes *acquaintance* as that source. What exactly is acquaintance? Here Fumerton gives us largely negative guidance:

Acquaintance is *not* another intentional state to be construed as a nonrelational property of the mind. [13]

Acquaintance is a sui generis *relation* that holds between a self and a thing, property, or fact. [13]

To be acquainted with a fact is not *by itself* to have any kind of propositional knowledge or justified belief. [13]

One can be acquainted with a property or fact without even possessing the conceptual resources to *represent* that fact in thought. [13]

Acquaintance is a relation that other animals probably bear to properties and even facts, but it also probably does not give these animals any kind of justification for believing anything, precisely because these other animals probably do not have beliefs. [13]

When one is acquainted with a fact, the fact is *there* before consciousness. Nothing stands "between" the self and the fact. [14]

Fumerton's proposal is then:

Fumerton's Principle
One has a noninferentially justified belief that P when one has the thought that P and one is acquainted with the fact that P, the thought that P, and the relation of correspondence holding between the thought that P and the fact that P.

He explains this proposal by saying

When everything that is *constitutive* of a thought's being true is immediately before consciousness, there is nothing more that one could want or need to justify a belief. [14]

I am not just being philosophically coy when I say that I am not sure what Fumerton means by "acquaintance." For example, what are the candidates for P in Fumerton's principle? Can one be acquainted with facts about the external world by virtue of perceiving it, or is one only acquainted with facts about percepts, appearances, or what have you?

Fumerton answers this question by saying that it is his view that it is always a mental state or feature of a mental state with which we are acquainted. This implies that when I see a red object, it is not the red object with which I am acquainted but rather a red percept. So on this view my noninferentially justified belief would be about a percept.

I am not sure how to rectify this with the requirement that we be acquainted with the relation of correspondence holding between the thought that P and the fact that P. Perhaps this counts as a "feature of a mental state," but I am unsure of what it is to be acquainted with such a feature. The only possibility I can think of is that simply by virtue of having the thought one is acquainted with the correspondence because the correspondence is merely a matter of the thought having the content it does. But if this is right, then this clause of Fumerton's principle is automatically satisfied and so we can omit it, leaving us with the simpler principle:

> One has a noninferentially justified belief that P when one has the thought that P and one is acquainted with the fact that P and the thought that P.

Now let us focus on what it is to be acquainted with a percept. Can one have a percept without being acquainted with it? Similarly, can one have a thought without being acquainted with it? If in both cases the answer is "No," then Fumerton's principle reduces to the principle he has already rejected, according to which simply having the percept justifies one in thinking one has the percept. So presumably Fumerton thinks we can have a percept without being acquainted with it. But what more is required? The only possibility I can think of is that acquaintance with a percept requires focus of attention on the percept. But in normal perceptual situations we do not focus our attention on percepts. Our attention is focused on the objects in the physical world that we are perceiving. So this would seem to imply that we do not usually have the noninferentially justified beliefs that Fumerton's foundationalism would require in order for us to be justified in holding other beliefs about physical objects, and hence *we should not hold those beliefs*. Fumerton actually flirts with such a view in his conclusion, but surely these beliefs are stereotypical examples of the kind of beliefs it is reasonable to hold, at least in a procedural sense of epistemic justification.

I am not at all sure that I have understood Fumerton's theory. But if my tentative suggestions regarding how to understand "acquaintance" are right, then I think his theory comes down to saying that having a percept can justify a belief to the effect that one has it. I think that is probably true, although Fumerton himself explicitly rejects it. Perhaps this will all become a little clearer when I turn to BonJour's theory. One thing that is clear is that Fumerton's positive theory is not a version of doxastic foundationalism. The foundations seem to consist of states of acquaintance, which are taken to justify beliefs about percepts, and they in turn justify other beliefs in some traditional foundationalist way.

IV. BonJour

BonJour follows Fumerton in taking foundationalism, at least of the sort he is interested in defending, as having a foundational structure and being internalist. BonJour takes foundationalism to require foundational beliefs, where

> A foundational . . . belief is supposed to be an empirical belief that (a) is adequately justified in the epistemic sense, but (b) whose epistemic justifica tion does not depend on inference from further empirical beliefs that would in turn have to be somehow justified. [22-23]

The fundamental problem for the foundationalist is how foundational beliefs get justified. BonJour's answer is that they "are justified by appeal to *experience*," [23] in a sense that must be explained. His explanation, reminiscent of Fumerton, is in terms of acts of "direct apprehension" or "direct acquaintance." He, like Fumerton, begins by taking the Sellarsian dilemma seriously:

> If it is construed as cognitive and conceptual, having as its content something like the proposition or claim that the experience in question has the specific character indicated by the belief, then it is easy to see how this second mental act can, if it *is itself justified*, provide a reason for thinking that the belief is true, but it is hard to see why it does not itself require justification . . . If, on the other hand, the mental act of direct apprehension . . . is construed as noncognitive, . . . it becomes difficult to see how such an act of direct apprehension can provide any reason or other basis for thinking that the original allegedly foundational belief is true. [23-24]

Like Fumerton, BonJour proposes to resolve the dilemma by acknowledging that the requisite direct apprehension is noncognitive and nonconceptual, but explaining how it can nevertheless justify beliefs about percepts.

BonJour gives a two-stage argument, first addressing beliefs about beliefs, and then turning to beliefs about percepts, but I will just focus on the latter. BonJour's suggestion is that a percept is a *conscious state*, and what this means is that

> it automatically involves a constitutive or "built-in," nonapperceptive awareness of its own distinctive sort of content, namely, sensory or experiential content. [29]

> Such a constitutive awareness of sensory content is in no need of justification and is indeed infallible in the sense that there is no sort of mistake that is even relevant to it. [29]

So the claim is (1) that whenever we have a percept we also have an awareness of its content, and (2) that awareness is nonconceptual.

In order to resolve the Sellarsian dilemma, BonJour must explain how this awareness can justify the belief that we have such a percept. His answer has two parts. First, given the nonconceptual nature of the intrinsic awareness, it cannot be *logically* connected with the belief that we have the percept. Instead, the connection is *descriptive*. And second, "the character of the nonconceptual object can obviously constitute a kind of reason or basis for thinking that the description is true or correct," provided we have "some sort of independent access to the character of the nonconceptual item, that is, an access that does not depend on the conceptual description itself." [30] BonJour concludes:

> Thus where I have a conscious state of sensory experience, I am, as already argued, aware of the specific sensory content of that state simply by virtue of having that experience. And thus if an apperceptive belief that I entertain purports to describe . . . that perceptual content, . . . and if I understand the descriptive content of that belief, . . . then I seem to be in a good, indeed an

ideal, position to judge whether the conceptual description is accurate, . . . and if so, to be thereby justified in accepting the belief. [30]

This theory is strikingly similar to Fumerton's. We can regard it as an attempt to explain the concept of acquaintance as it occurs in Fumerton's theory.

But now, let us look more closely at this concept of intrinsic awareness. The wedge into BonJour's theory is through the claim that having a percept is a conscious state, and conscious states have associated with them an intrinsic awareness of their content. First, there is some reason to doubt that having a percept is always a conscious state. There is psychological evidence to the effect that one aspect of short term memory is concerned with the recollection of visual appearances. Furthermore, when a subject is attending closely to a particular part of his visual field, he may be completely unaware of the contents of some other distant part of his visual field—unaware both of how things look in that part of his field and of the part of his environment that is represented by that part of his field—but if the light is extinguished and the subject is quickly asked about how things looked in that part of his visual field, he can often tell us. This strongly suggests that the subject had a percept representing that part of the field but was unaware of it at the time he had it. He only became aware of it by recalling it.

It is probably inessential to BonJour's theory to claim that having a percept is always a conscious state. It appears that all he need claim is that when a person bases a perceptual judgment on a percept, the percept is conscious and the consciousness involves having an intrinsic awareness of the content of the percept. The concept of a conscious state is sufficiently unclear that I am unsure how to adjudicate the claim that when one bases a perceptual judgment on a percept, the percept is conscious, so I will just focus on the claim that when one makes a perceptual judgment one is aware of the content of the percept.

What is it to be aware of the content of a percept? Does this require that one is aware *that* one has a percept with that content? I do not know how to understand such an awareness except as a belief. At the very least it seems to be the kind of conceptual act, having a propositional content, that BonJour is concerned to avoid. So I assume that we should not take being aware of the content of a percept to require being aware that one has a percept with that content.

I think there is something importantly right about the claim that when you see the world around you, you are aware of the content of your percept. You see the world "through your percept." The percept plays a representational role in your thought. It is by virtue of having the percept that you are able to think of features of the world in the way you do. To have a visual percept is to be presented with visual representations of objects and features of the world. When this happens, you do not think of the objects *by reference to* the percept, for example, as "the object represented by this percept." Rather, *having the percept* is a way of thinking of the objects. Your awareness is not *of the percept*—it is *of the objects you see* by virtue of having the percept.

This can be made more precise. On this view, the percept represents a (possible) state of affairs in the world. We can take that state of affairs to be the content of the percept. When perception is veridical, by virtue of having the percept one is aware of an instantiation of the state of affairs. We might also say something like: when perception is not veridical, by virtue of having the percept one is aware of a *putative* instantiation of the state of affairs. (Or we might say there is a merely putative awareness, but I will not pursue this.)

One might balk at the details of what I have just proposed, but I think this much is clear. When one perceives an object by having a percept, what one is normally aware of is the object, not the percept itself. One *can* become aware of the percept, but as I have repeatedly observed, that requires a deliberate change of attention.

So I am agreeing with BonJour that, at least in an ordinary perceptual situation, when one has a percept one is in a certain sense aware of its content. Will this awareness do the job BonJour wants? He argued:

> Where I have a conscious state of sensory experience, I am . . . aware of the specific sensory content of that state simply by virtue of having that experience. And thus if an apperceptive belief that I entertain purports to describe . . . that perceptual content, . . . I seem to be in a good, indeed an ideal, position to judge whether the conceptual description is accurate. [30]

However, the case in which I have an apperceptive belief about my percept is not a normal case of perception. This is a case in which I have focused my attention on the percept instead of the state of the world it represents. In such a case I become aware of the percept itself by introspecting it. It is tempting to say, on analogy to ordinary perception, that I become aware of the percept by having an introspective percept of the percept. But I will not push that. What is crucial is that the kind of awareness you have *of* the percept is quite different from the kind of awareness the percept itself provides in a normal perceptual situation.

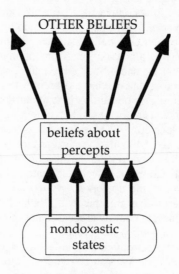

Figure 3.1

BonJour's argument seems to be trading on an equivocation of "awareness *of* the content of the percept" and "awareness *that* the percept has that content." The latter seems to be a straightforward belief—in fact, the very apperceptive belief whose justification is at issue. And, of course, I cannot judge whether the conceptual description of my percept is correct just by appealing to the belief that it is. That would be circular.

The conclusion I want to draw from this is that the observation that having a percept normally involves having an awareness of its content is an important observation about mental representation, but it will not do the job BonJour wants it to do in explaining how apperceptive beliefs about percepts are justified. To argue otherwise, BonJour will have to argue that having a percept involves an awareness of its content in some other sense than the one I have articulated, but I do not see what that sense is.

V. Nondoxastic Foundationalisms

Traditional foundationalism takes the foundations to consist of foundational beliefs. That is, it is doxastic foundationalism. The foundationalist theories defended by Fumerton and BonJour are both nondoxastic foundationalisms. They take the foundations to consist of states of acquaintance or direct awareness. They argue that these nondoxastic states justify beliefs about our percepts, which in turn can be used to justify other beliefs. Such foundationalist theories look much like traditional foundationalist theories in that there is a lowest level of beliefs, on the basis of which all other beliefs are justified, but unlike traditional foundationalist theories, the beliefs in this lowest level do not represent the ultimate foundation for justification—that is provided by nondoxastic states. We could diagram such a theory as in figure 3.1.

I too have defended a nondoxastic foundationalism, but mine differs importantly from those of Fumerton and BonJour in that, for me, beliefs about physical objects can be (and usually are) justified directly by having percepts and without the justification passing through intermediary beliefs about percepts. See figure 3.2. On my account, we *can* form beliefs about percepts, and when we do they can be relevant to our judgments about physical objects, but we do not *have* to form such beliefs.

The argument for an account like mine and against an account of the sort proposed by Fumerton and BonJour is the one I gave earlier. In ordinary perceptual situations, people do not have beliefs about the way things look to them. The percepts they have represent putative states of affairs in the world, and by virtue of having those percepts it becomes defeasibly reasonable to believe that the world is as represented. In such cognition, there is no need to think about the percepts—we need only think about the world *in terms of* the percepts. And in fact, in ordinary perception it would be detrimental to the functioning of a cognitive agent to require it to think about the percepts. We have limited cognitive capacity, and to require continual conscious monitoring of our cognitive processes in the acquisition of perceptual knowledge of the world would consume cognitive resources unnecessarily. On the other hand, it is important that we *can*

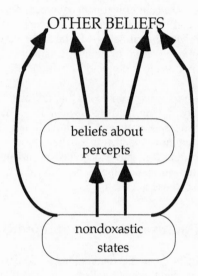

Figure 3.2

introspectively monitor our percepts in special cases, because perception is not always reliable and it is desirable to be able to discover the kinds of cases in which it is not reliable and block the inferences in those cases.

In supposing that perceptual knowledge must always pass through beliefs about percepts, I think that Fumerton and BonJour are being driven by what I called "the over-intellectualization of cognition." They are supposing that rational thought must be directed by deliberate decisions about what to believe, and that in turn leads them to suppose that there must be something that justifies the move from percepts to beliefs. As I observed earlier, if these deliberate decisions about what to believe are themselves rational, then on this account we must also decide deliberately how to go about deciding deliberately, and we are off and running on an infinite regress. This is just a bad model of cognition. We have to allow most of our cognitive processes to proceed automatically, without any monitoring or deliberate direction or intervention, but leave a place for monitoring and intervention when it is useful. Once it is realized that this is how cognition must work, there is nothing remarkable about the idea that in perception we move directly from percepts to beliefs about physical objects, and this is a stereotypical example of rational cognition. This move does not require justification. It must be an irreducible component in a competence theory of cognition. In other words, it must be a primitive part of a correct theory of procedural epistemic justification, and partially constitutive of rationality.[5]

Notes

1. And earlier in Pollock 1974.

2. Goodman 1955. The version of the Nicod Principle in question proposes that sets of premises of the form "$(Ac \ \& \ Bc)$" confirm the generalization "All A's are B's," for any choice of A and B.

3. This is not to say that everyone is equally good at cognizing. Cognitive performance varies dramatically. But insofar as people make cognitive mistakes, they can generally be brought to recognize them as such, suggesting that their underlying procedural knowledge is the same.

4. This volume, p. 3. Henceforth references to pages within this volume will be made in the text in square brackets.

5. It remains to give a precise formulation of the epistemic norms governing the inference from percepts to beliefs about the external world. This is clearly a defeasible inference, and the general logical theory of this and other defeasible inferences is investigated in detail in Pollock 1995.

Chapter 4

Direct Acquaintance?

Alvin Plantinga

When I first read BonJour's very interesting paper, I thought he supported a brand of foundationalism according to which in order to be justified in believing a proposition P—*any* proposition P—I must have a *reason* for so believing, a reason for thinking P is true, a reason with respect to which it is likely that P is true. Now I see that this is not what he means at all. He means to say that I can be justified in believing (e.g.) that I am being appeared to redly even if there is no other belief on the evidential basis of which I hold this belief. I am justified just by virtue of the very experience itself, which is an awareness of a certain sensuous content. But *how* does this awareness justify my belief that I am being appeared to redly? One might suspect, here, that the previous notion of justification—having a reason for the justified belief—still plays a surreptitious part. That is because of an ambiguity with respect to the term 'awareness': on the one hand there is awareness *of* the content, which of course is not a reason for believing anything; it simply is not the right kind of animal to be a reason, since it is not itself a belief or acceptance of a proposition. On the other hand, there is the awareness *that* I am being appeared to thus and so; this awareness is indeed constituted by a belief, but the belief in question is the very belief whose justification we seek, and hence of course cannot justify it. I do not accuse BonJour of falling into this confusion, though I am not sure that he has avoided it. In any event this confusion lurks in the neighborhood and is nearly maximally seductive.

Still what *does* BonJour mean by 'justification'? As I originally understood him, a necessary condition of being justified in believing a proposition is to have a reason for thinking that proposition true. If we turn our backs on this condition, what *is* it to be justified? And how does the belief that I am being appeared to redly acquire justification? And why is it that the justification of any other empirical belief must rest on noninferential justification? I do not think BonJour's notion of justification is very directly connected with the original deontological notion of justification in Descartes and Locke; but then what is it? Something else he says gives a clue:

> And thus if an apperceptive belief that I entertain purports to describe or conceptually characterize that perceptual content, albeit no doubt incompletely, and if I understand the descriptive content of that belief, i.e., understand what an experience would have to be like in order to satisfy the conceptual descrip-

tion, then I seem to be in a good, indeed, ideal position to judge whether the conceptual description is accurate as far as it goes, and if so, to be thereby justified in accepting the belief. [30]

Here it looks as if I am justified in holding this belief noninferentially if I am in *a good condition,* or maybe an *ideally* good condition to judge whether the description is accurate, i.e., whether it is true that I am being appeared to redly. This is not because I simply cannot be mistaken here: "Here again there is no reason to think that mistake is impossible and thus no reason to think that such an apperceptive belief is infallible or indubitable." [30] So what justifies me here is not that the belief in question is one I cannot be mistaken about. Perhaps I can make a mistake; nevertheless I am in a good or ideal condition or position to tell whether the proposition is true. (Would this be because there is high objective probability of its being true, given that I believe it? How would one know a thing like that?) If that is sufficient for noninferential justification, however, why cannot I also be justified in believing noninferentially that the chair before me is red? Am I not also in a good, even ideal position to make that judgment? My eyesight is excellent; the light is good; I am standing only a couple of feet from the chair; and so on. Well, perhaps my position here is not *ideally* good, at least if that requires that its goodness be unexcelled. Perhaps I am in a better position to judge that 2+1=3, or that I am being appeared to redly. But is not my position with respect to judging whether there is a chair present, at least a *good* position? And is not that good enough to have noninferential justification? It is not as if I were 400 yards away, or the light were bad, or I had lost my glasses. Of course it might be that BonJour thinks one can be noninferentially justified only if one is in a *maximally* good position: but then why think that?

I will return to this question in a moment; first, a few words about Fumerton. Of course Fumerton's essay is trenchant, deep, carefully crafted, and tightly packed, not the sort of essay about which one can be responsible or (as it were) justified in saying just a few offhand words. But why let a little thing like that stand in our way?

Fumerton also believes that there are noninferentially justified beliefs and that all justified beliefs owe their justification, ultimately, at least in part, to the existence of noninferentially justified beliefs. Since Fumerton gives us license to construe the notion of justification as that of warrant, I am in enthusiastic agreement with him here. Second, Fumerton thinks that properly basic beliefs—i.e., noninferentially justified beliefs—are justified by virtue of a relation of *direct acquaintance.* This is a relation between a self and something else—a thing, a property, or a fact, as he says. And a belief P is properly basic—i.e., noninferentially justified—just if the believer is directly acquainted with three things: (a) the thought that P, (b) the fact that P, and (c) a certain relation of correspondence between the thought that P and the fact that P. None of these acquaintances by itself will do the trick; all three are needed for the belief that P to be noninferentially justified or warranted. And I take it that (a), the thought that P, is not just the *proposition* that P, but rather the fact that S is thinking P "in a belief mode" as Fumerton says; it is the state of affairs consisting in S's thinking of P in that way.

Fumerton does not think he can say a lot about this relation of acquaintance: "Because the relations of acquaintance and the correspondence the above account appeals to are sui generis, there is precious little one can say by way of trying to explain the concept to one who claims not to understand it." [14] I do not myself claim not to understand this concept, though I also do not myself claim that I *do* understand it. The concept is the concept of a certain kind of mental act, or rather relation; one that I think Fumerton thinks is introspectable, such that one can tell whether it holds by paying careful attention, perhaps *very* careful attention, to one's own experience. There may be several sorts of relations in the near neighborhood, and the one I *think* Fumerton is thinking of may or may not be the very one he *is* thinking of. Nonetheless I understand something of what Fumerton means by 'acquaintance', or perhaps have a grasp of something at least *similar* to what he thinks of as acquaintance. "When one is acquainted with a fact," he says, "the fact is *there* before consciousness. Nothing stands 'between' the self and the fact." [14] It does seem to me sensible to say that when one is appeared to redly, the fact that one is so appeared to is indeed there before consciousness, and nothing stands between the self and that fact.

But perhaps this relation of acquaintance extends further than Fumerton suggests. I should think the same would go at least for simple mathematical and logical facts: am I not acquainted, in this sense, with the fact that 2+1=3? When I consider that fact, nothing seems to stand between me and it; it is there before my consciousness. Indeed, cannot we go still further? I am now aware, I should say, of the fact that there is a chair before me: am I not directly acquainted with that fact? This fact in a certain way impresses itself upon me as I look at the chair; it presents itself to me; it forces itself upon me. I should say it—i.e., the fact, but also the chair—is there before my consciousness. True, I can be acquainted with this fact only if I am also appeared to in one of a certain range of characteristic ways: but perhaps those ways of being appeared to are just modes of presentation of the fact in question. I am so constituted that I can be acquainted with that fact only when being appeared to in those ways; those ways of being appeared to, however, do not stand *between* me and the fact; instead they *present* the fact to me. And in the same or similar way, cannot I be acquainted with facts about the past by way of memory? And perhaps facts about God by way of something like Calvin's *sensus divinitatis,* or some other cognitive process? True: the *chair* is a component or element of this fact (the fact that there is a chair before me), and the chair is not itself, so to speak, diaphanous to consciousness; there is much about it that I do not and probably could not even grasp. But of course the same goes for the fact that I am appeared to redly; this fact contains as a component or constituent I myself; and I myself am not diaphanous to consciousness, in that there is much about myself that I do not and probably could not even grasp.

I realize Fumerton will demur here although I am not really sure why. So the question I want to ask is this (and here I also come back to BonJour): why cannot I be directly acquainted with the chair, and with the fact that there is a chair before me, and with my perceiving the chair, thereby being justified in those beliefs? What is the crucial difference between the case of my being appeared to thus and so, and my actually perceiving the chair? Perhaps someone will say:

you cannot be acquainted with facts like *that*—facts about the chair; you can only be acquainted with facts such that what *makes the corresponding thought true* is right there, in or before consciousness. But I should think that what makes the relevant chair thought true, from Fumerton's perspective anyway, is the fact that there *is* a chair before me; that is the truth-maker for this proposition. And that fact, I should have thought, *is* indeed right there in or before consciousness.

BonJour suggested in discussion that the difference has to do with this: in the case of an awareness, what I am aware of *makes it likely* that the corresponding belief—that I am being thus appeared to—is true; not so in the chair case. But this cannot be quite right: my awareness is not *itself* something with respect to which a proposition can be probable, because it is not itself a proposition. On the other hand, the proposition that I *am* thus aware certainly makes probable the proposition in question, since it just *is* the proposition in question. And the same holds in the chair case: what I am aware of is the chair, and my being aware of the chair does indeed entail that I am aware of the chair.

I can think of only two kinds of possibly relevant differences. First, then, someone else might say,

> Look: the only sorts of facts you can actually be acquainted with are those that are *incorrigible* in something like the sense Pollock suggests: say that a proposition P is incorrigible for S at a time t if and only if S's paying careful attention to his phenomenal field and believing P at t entails that P is true, and his paying careful attention to his phenomenal field and believing not-P at t entails that not-P is true. So then you can be acquainted with the fact that you are appeared to redly, but not with the fact that there is a chair before you.

Now BonJour, as we saw, is not prepared to avail himself of this difference. And Fumerton too cannot avail himself of this suggestion, because he too apparently thinks nothing or next to nothing *is* incorrigible in this sense. I am sorry to say I was not at all convinced by the arguments for this conclusion Fumerton says are plausible. In one of these arguments you are asked to imagine a situation in which you think you are in pain—perhaps you have a severe toothache. You are wired to a machine that reliably detects neural activity; the technician tells you that there is no indication of the relevant neural activity; he concludes that you are *not* in pain. I do not know about you, but I think I would continue to believe that I am in pain. I would continue to believe that even if the machine indicated no neural activity at all, indeed, even if what it indicated was that I do not so much as *have* a brain. But actually this is not the issue; the question is really whether if, under those conditions, I *continued* to believe that I was in pain, I would *be* in pain. If I do stop believing that I am in pain because of what the machine says, then perhaps we should think of this machine as an exceptionally complicated anodyne, sort of like an unusually high tech aspirin. It gets me to believe that I am not in pain, which is sufficient for my not being in pain.

Fumerton also points out that my being in pain is *one* state of affairs, and my believing that I am in pain is *another*: how then, could the second entail the first? But of course there are many distinct states of affairs S and S*, such that S entails S*: for example, *7's being prime* and *7's being odd*, or *John's being 32 years old* and *John's being more than 10 years old*. No doubt Fumerton will reply that these states of affairs are not distinct in the relevant sense: but I doubt that the relevant sense can be specified without appealing to the notion of entailment, saying that S and S* are distinct in the relevant sense only if S does not entail S*.

So I am not convinced that there are no appropriately incorrigible mental states. Even if there are such incorrigible states, however, it is worth noting that my knowledge—acquired a priori, perhaps—*that* there are does not function to give me a reason for believing that I am in such a state. For suppose I knew a priori that I am in an excellent position to make the judgment; suppose, indeed, I knew that

(a)   judgments about how I am appeared to cannot be mistaken: necessarily, if I believe that I am being appeared to X-ly, I am being appeared to X-ly.

Would that give me a reason for the belief that I am being appeared to redly? No. For me to employ (a), I should have to know first that I *believe* that I am being appeared to redly, another judgment that requires justification. Well, then suppose we amend (a) so that it also specifies that my occurrent beliefs about my own occurrent beliefs are incorrigible:

(a*)   occurrent judgments about how I am appeared to or what I occurrently believe cannot be mistaken.

Would that help? No; to use (a*) I must now first know that

(b)   I believe that I believe that I am being appeared to redly.

Given (b) I can conclude by way of (a*), that I believe that I am being appeared to redly and hence (by (a)) really am being appeared to redly. But what is my justification for believing (b)? To draw that conclusion with the help of (a*) I should have to know first that

(c)   I believe that I believe that I believe that I am being appeared to redly.

It is obvious where this is going; (a*) does not help: it is always a day late and a dollar short; there is a sort of levels confusion involved in thinking one can justify the judgment that I am being appeared to redly by the use of (a*). Accordingly, as far as I can see there is not any sensible way in which my being appeared to redly can be the justification for my belief that I am thus appeared to; it cannot be itself a *reason* for my belief that I am being appeared to redly. That is because it is simply not the right sort of animal to serve as a reason: it is not itself a belief; it does not itself have a truth-value; it is not itself something from which something can be inferred; it does not itself possess propositional content. And once again, if we insist that nonetheless it *is* a reason, then I would be inclined to suggest that in the same way my awareness of this chair can serve as my reason for believing that I see a chair, and my awareness of God as my reason for believing that I am aware of God.

But suppose there are propositions of this sort that are also incorrigible for me: why should we think that a necessary condition of my being directly acquainted with a contingent fact is the corresponding proposition's being incorrigible for me? Of course we could just *stipulate* that it is: this, we can say, is just how we propose to use the technical term 'directly acquainted with'. But then we face the real question—the biggest question in this entire area, as it seems to me: why should we think that I can know or justifiably believe a proposition only if it is related, in the way the foundationalist suggests, to facts with which I am directly acquainted, in this technical sense of 'acquainted'? Why think acquaintance with facts in *that* sense must lie at the foundations of knowledge? Why think that if we recognize that our knowledge of the external world is not inferentially justified with respect to facts with which I am acquainted in that sense, then we must acquiesce in skepticism? I do not myself find this proposition plausible—or rather, I do not find it nearly as plausible as the proposition that I know such things as that there is a chair before me.

Fumerton proposes another way in which the possibility of error is relevant. Suppose you think that you are directly acquainted with the table: it would be plausible to think also that you *would have been* justified in believing that there is a table there, even if there *were* no table there, provided your experience were relevantly like what it is in fact. Now according to Fumerton,

> Nevertheless, arguments from the possibility of error still have a role to play in deciding with what we can be directly acquainted. If one concedes, for example, that the *justification* one now has for believing that there is a table before one is perfectly compatible with the table's not being there, then one has just conceded that one is not directly acquainted with the table. [16]

That is because if I am directly acquainted with the table, then my justification for believing that there is a table before me *includes* my being acquainted with the fact that the table is there. But of course I cannot be acquainted with the fact that the table is there unless indeed it *is* there; hence my justification—the justification I actually have—entails that the table is there. Hence it cannot be *both* that I am justified in believing that there is a table before me by way of being directly acquainted with the table, *and* that my justification is such that I would have had that *same* justification even if the table were not there.

So far so good. But how is this a reason for thinking that I cannot be directly acquainted with the table? Or rather, if it *is* a reason for that, then is not it also a reason for thinking that I cannot be directly acquainted with, e.g., the fact that I am being appeared to in a certain way? In the preceding paragraph Fumerton points out that

> Specifically, I have argued that one might be acquainted with a fact very similar to the fact that makes P true, and such acquaintance might give one a justified but false belief that P. [15]

For example, I might be noninferentially justified in believing that

(d)   I seem to see shade S of pink

when in fact I do not seem to see *that* shade of pink, but a shade S* very similar to S. This means that one can acquire a justified false noninferential belief to the effect that P, where P is a fact (or candidate for facthood) of the sort with which one can be acquainted. Now: suppose I am in fact directly acquainted with (d), the fact that I seem to see shade S of pink. Then my justification for thinking that (d) consists in part in my being acquainted with the fact that (d). But then I could not have *that same* justification for believing (d) if (d) were not in fact true: the situation is precisely like that in the case of alleged direct acquaintance with the fact that the table is present. So shouldn't I say the same thing in both cases? In both cases I can be justified in believing P even if P is false; but equally, in both cases, if I were justified in believing P when P is false, my justification would not be the same as it is when I am justified by being directly acquainted with P. If the possibility of error suggests the absence of direct acquaintance in the one case, it does the same in the other case.

I therefore suggest that I can be acquainted with such facts as that there is a chair before me. In *Warrant and Proper Function* (1993b) I argued that a belief is noninferentially warranted if and only if (roughly) it is not accepted on the evidential basis of other beliefs and is produced by properly functioning cognitive faculties according to a design plan successfully aimed at the production of true belief. Perhaps a belief that P meets these conditions for a person S if and only if S is noninferentially justified in accepting this belief in Fumerton's sense: i.e., if and only if S is acquainted with the belief that P, the fact that P, and the correspondence between them. This would be a pleasing meeting of minds.

Pollock

I find much to agree with in Pollock's comments. In particular, I am enthusiastic about the notion of procedural rationality, which I gloss as that of proper function. I would only comment that to wind up in the area of knowledge, one has to add something to the idea that the belief in question is true and has been arrived at by way of procedural rationality and proper function: one has to add that the bit of the cognitive design plan governing the production of the belief is successfully aimed at the production of true beliefs, not just beliefs with some other virtue.

One of Pollock's arguments, however, does require a bit of comment. He asks the question "Why should we accept the premise of this argument, according to which having a reason for a belief must consist of being in an intentional state?" [44] and then he criticizes a bad argument for that conclusion. Well, I agree: that argument is a bad argument. But next Pollock points out, presumably in an attempt to support that view, that I *could* have a reason for believing something where the reason did not consist in being in an intentional state, that *cognition*, as he says, can (metaphorically) take account of things other than beliefs, even if *I* do not: "However, it is *cognition* that must note that we have certain beliefs—*we* do not have to note it ourselves. The sense in which cognition notes it is metaphorical...." [44] I am not quite sure I understand this, but to the extent that I do, it does not seem to me to show that *I* can have a reason for believing something that is not itself a belief. For of course cognition does not really have beliefs, and does not have reasons for belief: people do. So even if my cognition (or cognition in me) takes account of something other than an intentional state, it does not follow that *I* thereby have a reason for believing something or other. (In *Contemporary Theories of Knowledge* (1987), Pollock explains *internal state* in such a way that blood pressure is an internal state. Perhaps, then, cognition somehow takes account of my high blood pressure; that does not as such give me a reason for the belief that I have high blood pressure.) It is only in a metaphorical or extended sense that something other than a belief can be a reason, for me, to believe or do something or other. You might tell me, "That noxious dump in your backyard is a good reason to move;" but it is not a good reason for me to move if, through rather striking inattention, I have not formed the belief that there *is* a dump in my backyard.

Part III

Replies

Chapter 5

Replies to Pollock and Plantinga

Richard Fumerton

Let me begin my replies to Pollock's and Plantinga's penetrating and insightful comments by trying to find at least one point of agreement. Pollock suggests that it has become increasingly apparent "that there is more than one important concept that might reasonably be called 'epistemic justification.'" [46] This seems exactly right to me, but I think Pollock (and many other contemporary epistemologists) have, ironically, left behind one very important concept of philosophically relevant justification. I have argued elsewhere (Fumerton 1995) that there is a concept of epistemic justification of particular interest to the philosopher who is engaged in what is, to be sure, a rather unusual activity. The demands of philosophically relevant justification are stronger than the demands of ordinary concepts of justification precisely because the philosopher is interested in a concept the satisfaction of which removes a kind of philosophical curiosity that prompts the raising of philosophical questions about justification in the first place.

To discover which beliefs are or are not justified in Pollock's sense of the term is ultimately to engage in a psychological investigation. For Pollock the question of whether or not a belief is justified is a function of which rules we follow with respect to belief formation. To say that we follow a certain epistemic rule licensing a certain inference is ultimately to assert a subjunctive conditional about which beliefs we would form under certain conditions. To be sure, Pollock will insist that the existence of these rules is not equivalent to "mere generalizations about how we cognize," [48] but he will, nevertheless, equate the existence of the relevant "normative" epistemic rules with facts, perhaps quite complicated facts, about how we would form beliefs under certain conditions, where these conditions include reference to the "self-correcting" dispositions he talks about in his comments. Discovering the rules that define which beliefs are or are not justified in this sense is, according to Pollock, analogous to discovering the syntactic rules we follow in putting words together to form sentences.

As I suggested in my paper, it is even misleading to characterize Pollock as an internal state internalist. According to Pollock for a belief to have the property of being justified is for a belief to have the property of being sanctioned by an appropriate belief-formation rule. This property is a complex property the exemplification of which involves factors far beyond the internal states of the subject. The only connection Pollock's concept of justification has to internal states is that the relevant rules always license inferences from internal states to doxastic states. But, of course, one could incorporate *this* idea into relatively straightforward versions of reliabilism. Indeed, it seems to me that Pollock's foundationalism is really better construed as a species of externalism, as a kind of reliabilism without a requirement of reliability! For Pollock the belief-forming "software" always operates on internal states, and there is no requirement that the relevant rules determining justified belief be such that following them usually gets us at the truth.

To argue against Pollock's view, I would have to explain my general reservations about externalist and naturalistic epistemologies, and this would take us somewhat far afield. It does, however, seem obvious to me that epistemologists who take seriously the challenge of skepticism, who think that the skeptic is raising important and interesting questions about whether we can find justification for our spontaneous and unreflective beliefs, are not working with Pollock's concept of justification. Skeptics are not wondering, for example, whether we are disposed to form beliefs about the external world when prompted by sensory states. This is the datum with which the skeptic starts. The interesting question is whether we are *justified* in forming such beliefs. Put in Pollock's terminology, the skeptic wants to know whether or not the rules we (often unreflectively) follow in forming beliefs are rules we epistemically should be following.[1] But Pollock's concept of justified belief ultimately won't allow the intelligibility of this question. As soon as it becomes evident to the traditional epistemologist that on Pollock's view the study of normative epistemology collapses into psychology, the traditional epistemologist will lose interest in the subject so-defined. If one is interested in whether or not the rules we follow in forming beliefs are *legitimate*, one will hardly be satisfied with an empirical investigation that employs (and thus implicitly presupposes the legitimacy of) those very rules.

Obviously, none of the above will faze Pollock. He is, no doubt, convinced that the traditional epistemologist is trying to ask a question that can't be asked. The traditional epistemologist, he will argue, wants somehow to step out from his belief-forming software and investigate it without using belief-forming software, and that is something that no one can do. The acquaintance theorist, however, is convinced that with respect to at least noninferentially justified belief, one can find a kind of justification that can satisfy in an ideal way the philosophical search for truth. The acquaintance theorist is convinced that with respect to some truths, one can be directly aware of both the truth-bearer and the truth-maker and the correspondence that defines truth. When one has all of the elements of truth directly before consciousness, there is nothing else one could want or need when it comes to having further or better justification.

Pollock argues that epistemologists "have a lamentable tendency to over-intellectualize cognition." [44] If he is talking about over-intellectualizing the actual process of forming beliefs he is, I think, quite right. If he is, however, claiming that philosophers over-intellectualize what is involved in finding philosophically satisfying justification for a belief, then I think he is quite wrong. Unfortunately, the two concepts have often been carelessly mixed by some in the history of epistemology. But not by everyone. David Hume not only realized, but emphasized, the spontaneous and unreflective character of ordinary beliefs. He famously speculated that nature has wisely not made our ability to form beliefs dependent on our ability to satisfy reason. But acknowledging this point is quite irrelevant to the question in which the philosopher is still interested: *Can* reason satisfy itself with respect to the beliefs we spontaneously and unreflectively form?

When the philosopher asks this question it is probably best to construe it as a question about whether there is *available* to us justification in support of what we believe. It is critical to distinguish there being justification for S to believe P and S's belief that P being justified. As many have pointed out, the latter concept probably requires that S's belief that P be caused by, or be causally sustained by, whatever justifies S in believing P (or at least by some *part* of what justifies S in believing P). My own view is that the question of which beliefs are or are not justified in this sense is of no real interest to philosophy. It is, after all, an *empirical* question as to what is causing or causally sustaining my beliefs and I do not think most epistemologists are competent to answer the question. It is once again a question more appropriately studied by psychologists, psychologists who presuppose in their psychological investigations answers to fundamental questions concerning what would count as legitimate evidence. The epistemologist engaged in normative epistemology should be content with settling questions about what could justify someone's belief (if the justification played the appropriate causal role in belief-formation).[2]

Keeping the above distinctions straight is important in assessing the relevance of Pollock's complaint that on traditional empiricist foundationalism, where the foundations of empirical knowledge are restricted to beliefs about mental contents, there are simply not enough of such beliefs to give us an appropriately robust foundation from which to infer the rest of what we believe. He *correctly* points out that people rarely have beliefs about how things appear. And if our justification for believing ordinary truths about the physical world ultimately consists in truths about how we are appeared to, then it would seem to follow that most people rarely have justified beliefs about the physical world.

I have already suggested that the epistemologist should not be primarily interested in the question of whether or not people have justified beliefs, particularly when the justification we are talking about is philosophically relevant justification. Again, however, I agree with Pollock that there are many concepts of justification and if one wants to allow derivative concepts of justified belief, where the justified belief does not have to be causally sustained by *belief* in the evidence available to justify it, I have no quarrel with doing so. In fact, years ago (Fumerton 1976), I suggested a way of doing precisely that. Crudely, one could allow an ordinary concept of justification where one allows a belief about the external world to be inferentially justified when it is caused by a sensory state which is the truth-maker for a proposition which is a part of the evidence from which we could legitimately infer the proposition. The psychology of the belief formation need not involve any conscious (or unconscious) inferences from beliefs about sensory states to beliefs about the physical world, even if it is also true that philosophical reflection will force us to the conclusion that the only way to find philosophically relevant justification for such beliefs is to turn our attention to the character of our sensory states. In philosophy of science there is an old, but still very important, distinction between the context of discovery and the context of justification. And there is an analogous distinction with respect to everyday beliefs concerning the way in which they were *caused* and what we can come up with by way of intellectually satisfying justification.

So I agree completely with Pollock that we relatively rarely form beliefs about the character of our sensations. I am not even sure how often we are directly acquainted with the detailed nonrelational character of our sensations. In this respect I want to disagree slightly with BonJour. Our views are now closely allied, but as I understand BonJour, he wants to argue that our direct awareness or acquaintance with the sensuous content of our sensory states is *constitutive* of those states. I am not sure in the end that I really understand that view. To be sure, sometimes BonJour puts the point in terms of what is essential to *conscious* mental states, and if by conscious mental states one just means mental states of which one is aware, then it is trivially true that there could not be a conscious mental sate of which one is unaware—one couldn't be unaware of a state of which one is aware. But if one is trying to characterize an ordinary mental state like pain, then I am not sure there is any conceptual difficulty in imagining my having a pain of which I am unaware. Indeed, one of the thought experiments through which I tried to "ostend" the concept of direct awareness involved my asking you to reflect on that pain of which you were keenly aware, but of which you became temporarily unaware while engaged in interesting conversation. It seems to me that for pains and all other sensory states, one can distinguish ontologically and conceptually the experiential state from the awareness of that state. And if one could not, one might face a vicious regress. After all, the experiential state Y, that according to BonJour *consists* of a sensory content, S, plus awareness of said content, A, is itself, presumably, an experiential state. But it cannot, by itself, *be* an experiential state because such states always have as a constituent awareness of the state. So the original sensory state must now be construed as S+A+A* (where A* is the awareness of S+A). But S+A+A* can't be an experiential state either without awareness of it, and so on ad infinitum. Every experiential state would seem to involve an infinite complexity. In light of this threatening regress it seems to me best to embrace the more modest position that our sensory states are often accompanied by our awareness of them, and, of course trivially, all of the ones of which we are aware are accompanied by our awareness of them.

So if I am right, ordinary beliefs about the physical world may be caused by sensory states about which we have no beliefs and may even be caused by such states when we have no direct acquaintance with those states. Again, none of this seems to me of any interest to the epistemologist wondering whether it would be best to construe the available evidence in support of beliefs about the physical world as consisting in what we *could come to know* about the character of our sensations.

But that does raise the question to which both Pollock and Plantinga want an answer. Why should we think that the only empirical beliefs which are noninferentially justified are beliefs about the character of our sensations? Pollock, I think, ultimately rejects the intelligibility of the concept of direct acquaintance in terms of which both BonJour and I want to define noninferential justification. Plantinga, on the other hand, seems prepared to extend, at least tentatively, an olive branch to those of us who want to ground noninferential justification in direct awareness or acquaintance, but still wonders why we direct acquaintance theorists are so stingy when it comes to allowing direct acquaintance with various sorts of phenomena. It seems to Plantinga that in whatever sense the pain I feel is "there" directly before consciousness, so too is the chair I see right now. Why should we say that one can have direct awareness of the pain but not of the chair?

Before answering this question I should, perhaps, remove some potential misunderstandings concerning my view. Plantinga suggests that "this relation of acquaintance extends further than Fumerton suggests." He goes on to ask if he is not "acquainted, in this same sense, with the fact that 2+1=3?" [61] In fact, I agree completely that one can be directly acquainted with the truth-makers for simple arithmetical truths, logical truths, and some synthetic necessary truths (e.g., equilateral triangles are equiangular triangles). In my paper I suggested only that "when one has noninferential justification for believing a *contingent* proposition the relevant acts of acquaintance will involve constituents all of which are 'internal' to the subject." [17, emphasis added.] Of course, before we decide what precisely it is, acquaintance with which yields direct knowledge of certain necessary truths, we will need to be clear about the truth-makers for necessary truths. If the British empiricists were correct, at least many necessary truths were made true by "relations between ideas." Given this view, one still does not need to be acquainted with anything beyond mental states (and relations holding between them) in order to get noninferential justification for believing certain necessary truths. Such a view is hardly unproblematic, however, and if one holds that the truth-makers for necessary truths are relations between Platonic propositions or universals, for example, and one is determined to ground direct knowledge of such truths in acquaintance, then one will need to convince oneself that one can be directly acquainted with Platonic propositions, universals, and relations that hold between them (as the Russell of *Problems of Philosophy*, 1912, did).

I do not propose to address the question of what makes necessary truths true and, consequently, what one must be acquainted with in order to know noninferentially a necessary truth. I would, however, suggest that it is one of the great *strengths* of an acquaintance theory that it has the resources to provide a *unified* account of noninferential justification. On classical acquaintance theories, the nature of our justification for believing both that we are in pain, when we are, and that 2+1=3, is direct acquaintance with the relevant fact that makes these respective thoughts true. To be sure, throughout the history of epistemology, most philosophers have sought to mark a crucial distinction between so-called a posteriori knowledge of contingent propositions (such as the proposition that I am in pain), and a priori knowledge of necessary truths such as that 2+1=3. But crude characterizations of this distinction are almost always hopelessly misleading. A posteriori knowledge rests on experience, while a priori knowledge does not? That's absurd. A priori knowledge clearly rests on experience of *something*, namely whatever the subject matter of a necessary truth is. One can suggest that a priori knowledge doesn't rest on *sense* experience, but then neither does my knowledge that I believe that grass is green rest on *sense* experience. An acquaintance theorist will argue that the critical difference between direct knowledge of contingent truths and direct knowledge of necessary truths does not lie in a difference between the source of such knowledge, but rather lies in a difference between the objects with which one is directly acquainted. And again, how different those objects are depends on one's account of what makes a necessary truth true.

But let us return to the main issue which seems to separate Plantinga from BonJour and me. Why should one deny that one is directly aware of ordinary, bread-box-sized physical objects when one seems to be perceiving them under what seems to be optimal conditions of perception? As Plantinga notes, I want to argue that it has something to do with the fact that we can have the *same* justification for believing that the table is there when hallucinating or vividly dreaming as we have when we veridically perceive a table. Since in the case of hallucinations and dreams we are not directly acquainted with the table (there is no table there to stand as one of the relata of the relation of awareness), then in the case of veridical perception we cannot hold that the justification consists of direct awareness of the table either. But as Plantinga reminds me, I have, perhaps unfortunately, allowed that one can have a noninferentially justified false belief. Although it has never been completely obvious to me what to say about this, I have somewhat reluctantly conceded that one can have noninferential justification for believing that one is in a certain sensory state, where that justification consists in the fact that one is directly acquainted with a different, but *very similar* sensory state. I might add, parenthetically, that with respect to *some* acts of direct acquaintance, it's not clear to me that there is any realistic possibility of confusing one fact with which I am acquainted with some other fact—I happen to agree with Plantinga that the thought experiment Armstrong appealed to is ultimately unconvincing in leading us to the conclusion that our noninferential justification for believing that we are in pain can be defeated. But I did allow for the possibility of noninferentially justified false belief. For example, I think that I might be noninferentially justified in believing that I seem to see twenty-five rectangular spots in my visual field by virtue of my direct acquaintance with what turns out to be twenty-six rectangular spots in my visual field.

After allowing that one can be noninferentially justified in believing a false proposition, why should the possibility of vivid hallucinatory experience cast doubt on the possibility of being noninferentially justified in believing that the table is there before me now. To be sure, if I can get Plantinga to admit that in both veridical and hallucinatory experience I would have *precisely the same* justification for believing that the table was there, he will concede, I think, that in the case of veridical experience we cannot construe that justification as direct awareness of a table. If direct awareness is a real relation (not an intentional state), then to be directly aware of a table is to stand in that relation to an existent table, but in hallucinatory experience there is no table there of which I can be aware. Again, since the justification I have for thinking that the table is there in hallucinatory experience is the same as the justification I have in veridical experience, then in veridical experience I am not directly aware of the table either.

But why should Plantinga concede that in both veridical and hallucinatory experience I have precisely the same justification for thinking that the table is there? After all, I have conceded that one can have noninferential justification for believing the true proposition that one is in a sensory state S, and also have noninferential justification for believing a false proposition that one is in a sensory state S. In the latter, the noninferential justification cannot consist in one's being directly acquainted with the fact that one is state S—by hypothesis that state does not exist. That noninferential justification, I have argued, must consist in my being directly aware of a state very similar to, and easily confused with, S. But then why can we not say the same thing about hallucinatory and veridical experience of the table? In the case of a vivid hallucinatory experience, I am directly acquainted with some fact that is easily confused with the existence of a table, whereas in veridical experience I am directly acquainted with the very fact that makes true the proposition I believe.

It should come as no surprise, here, that I will put all of the emphasis on the concept of one fact being easily confused with another. It may depend, in part, on one's ontological analysis of facts about the physical world, but on the face of it, the fact that there is a table before me now is nothing like any fact that is "before me" in a vivid dream or hallucination. (So as not to muddy the waters, I am assuming that in the dream or hallucination I am in an environment entirely unlike the environment I take myself to be in). What is the common or similar constituent supposed to be of my being directly acquainted with a table in veridical experience, and whatever it is that I am supposed to be directly acquainted with in hallucinatory experience? It seems patently obvious to me that there is a common (nondisjunctive!) phenomenologically given constituent of both veridical and hallucinatory experience, but the only plausible candidate for that common constituent is something like a sense datum or a way of being appeared to. It is, upon reflection, *that* with which we can be directly acquainted in both veridical and hallucinatory experience. But sense data and ways of being appeared to are not physical objects *and they are nothing like physical objects*. I cannot see how one could reasonably confuse a sense datum or an appearing with a fact about the physical world (in the way in which one might confuse one sensory state with another that differs only very subtly from the former).

Again, a full defense of this view would involve a more detailed conceptual analysis of propositions describing the physical world and their relation to propositions describing sensation. I can imagine, I suppose, a metaphysics which might try to close the phenomenological gap between veridically perceived physical objects and "hallucinatory physical objects." If one were a Meinongean, for example, who thought that there are objects (like tables) which exist, and those which do not, or who thought that there are states of affairs (like a table's being before one), some of which obtain and some of which do not, *and* if one thought that existent and nonexistent objects, obtaining and nonobtaining states of affairs are in some sense very similar and easily confused with one another, then one might have the resources from within the framework of an acquaintance theory to allow noninferential justification of physical object propositions in both veridical and nonveridical experience. It is hard for me to say because I would not touch such a metaphysics with a ten-foot pole. Even so, I would have thought that however the Meinongean understands the difference between existing and nonexisting objects, or obtaining and nonobtaining states of affairs, that difference would be enormous! And if it is, I would still want some explanation of how one could be phenomenologically unable to distinguish the existent from the nonexistent or the obtaining from the nonobtaining when, by hypothesis, one is directly aware of both.

To explore the epistemological implications of metaphysical analyses a bit further, consider a situation in which Plantinga will no doubt claim to be noninferentially justified in thinking that something has a certain color, say red. As we all know, a great many philosophers in the history of philosophy have claimed that physical redness (as opposed to phenomenal redness) is a secondary property of physical objects. For an object to be red is for the object to appear red to a normal observer under standard conditions. Now if red is a secondary property so-construed, then what would be involved in being directly acquainted with the fact that some physical object is red? One would need to be directly acquainted with the truth-maker for the relevant subjunctive conditional. On some views, this sort of contingent subjunctive conditional is made true, in part, by the existence of laws. And on some views, laws are made true by regularities that obtain, past, present and future. And even an extreme libertarian with respect to what we can be acquainted with must surely hesitate before claiming that one can be directly acquainted with regularities extending through time. Why? Because whatever justification we have for supposing that such regularities obtain would be precisely the same as the justification we have for supposing that such regularities obtain when they do not, and when they do not it is hardly plausible to claim that the justification consists in direct awareness of the regularities!

All of the above would constitute an argument against direct awareness of physical color only if one adopted that particular metaphysical analysis of what it is to have a color. My only concern here is to emphasize that the plausibility of a claim to be directly aware of a certain fact will often depend on the plausibility of a certain view about the constituents of that fact. It seems to me that on any plausible view about the facts that make true propositions asserting the existence of physical objects, such facts will be exceedingly complex in a way that makes quite impossible direct awareness of them.

Notes

1. In talking about what one epistemically *should* do, I might seem to be presupposing that epistemic questions are in some important sense normative. That there is an epistemic "should" seems to me undeniable. That it has much, if anything, to do with the paradigm "should" of normative moral judgments is a much more problematic claim. In fact, I have argued elsewhere (1995, Chapter 1) that it is a serious mistake to try to illuminate epistemic concepts by exploring parallels between them and the normative concepts of ethical theory.

2. The distinction I appeal to here applies to both inferential and noninferential justification. It might sound a bit odd to speak of someone's having available noninferential justification which does not causally sustain a belief, but in fact I think one

can indeed be directly acquainted with the kind of fact that could provide one with noninferential justification for believing some proposition P even when the belief that P is causally sustained by some factor other than the relevant direct acquaintance.

Chapter 6

Replies to Pollock and Plantinga

Laurence BonJour

To Pollock

It is not obvious to me how much genuine disagreement there is between Pollock's views and my own. Rather than a substantive disagreement, the main difference between us appears to me to be simply that we are pursuing substantially different projects.[1]

Pollock's project is to describe the epistemic norms that characterize our "built-in procedural knowledge of how to cognize," [48] i.e., I take it, the rules or norms, whether innate or learned, that we actually follow in our commonsensical cognitive activities. And in these terms he specifies a correlative notion of epistemic justification:

> A belief is justified in the procedural sense of epistemic justification just in case the cognition giving rise to it conforms to those norms. [48]

Thus if it is true, as it pretty plainly is, that we ordinarily arrive at perceptual beliefs about physical objects as a result of having sensory experience (or "percepts"[2]) without having any explicit beliefs about the content of that experience, and if doing so is not a violation of our ordinary, commonsense standards of rationality, then the beliefs thus arrived at are epistemically justified in this procedural sense.

I have no real quarrel with any of this (though there are obviously questions that could be asked about the precise nature and status of these commonsensical norms). But I have a different project in mind: the traditional project of what I will call *critical epistemology*, which asks whether we actually have or even could in principle have good reasons for thinking that our various beliefs are true, and construes epistemic justification as the possession of such reasons. Here "good reasons" means reasons that are genuinely cogent, not just ones that are commonsensically taken to be cogent.[3] (Thus what Pollock attempts to stigmatize as "the over-intellectualization of cognition" [56] is in fact essential to critical epistemology.) And hence the facts, already conceded, that we ordinarily move directly from the occurrence of sensory experience to beliefs about physical objects without having explicit beliefs about the content of the experience as such and that doing so is fully acceptable by our ordinary standards of rationality in no way settles the issue of whether beliefs arrived at in this way are justified in the critical epistemological sense (unless we simply assume that reasons which satisfy our ordinary standards are somehow guaranteed to be good ones, an assumption for which there seems to be no real basis).

My suggestion is thus that while the results of Pollock's procedural epistemology may perhaps be suggestive for critical epistemology, they have no stronger relevance than that. Instead the critical epistemological question of whether we have or could have good reasons for our beliefs about the physical world must be dealt with by actually considering and assessing the various possible accounts of what such reasons might amount to. My conviction, largely argued for elsewhere and taken for granted in the present paper, is that none of the familiar alternatives to foundationalism succeeds in giving an acceptable account of such reasons. Moreover, if the account of foundational beliefs that is argued for in this paper is right, then a view that would attribute foundational status to (some) beliefs about physical objects is also unacceptable. Thus I conclude that a satisfactory account of how beliefs about physical objects can be justified in the critical epistemological sense must involve an inference from foundational beliefs about the content of sensory experience, a view that seems to me to be strongly buttressed by the fact that the various details of that experience are clearly highly relevant, though in a way that urgently needs to be further elucidated, to our holding the specific beliefs about the physical world that we in fact hold. I have conceded in the paper that reasons or justification of this sort are not explicitly present in the minds of ordinary believers, though it does not seem to me implausible to say that they are available at least in principle to such believers—and also perhaps that such reasons can be regarded as something like a rational reconstruction of commonsense cognitive processes that are less critical and less reflective in character. (It is also obvious that explicitly formulating full reasons of the sort in question would in general be quite impossible from a practical standpoint; but this point also has no clear relevance to the issue with which critical epistemology is concerned.)

If the aspects of Pollock's discussion that merely reflect this difference in project are set aside, the only remaining differences that I can find between us concern a series of issues having to do with the content of sensory experience and our awareness thereof, issues that are at least partly phenomenological in character. Some of them are substantially more important than others, but it will be clearer to consider each of them in the order in which Pollock brings them up.

First. Pollock argues [53] that having a "percept," which I will understand as being in a state of sensory experience, is not always a conscious state. As he notes, there is nothing about my view that requires me to say that such experiential states are always conscious, as opposed to saying merely that only the conscious ones can be the subject of properly foundational beliefs. But the reason he offers for the claim that a state of sensory experience is not always conscious strikes me as both mistaken and misleading in a way that suggests that the range of such foundational beliefs is much more restricted than it is.

The reason in question is that

when a subject is attending closely to a particular part of his visual field, he may be completely unaware of the contents of some other distant part of his visual field—both of how things look in that part of his field and of the part of his environment that is represented by that part of his field.... [53]

While I would not want to insist that something like this might not be true in some sufficiently unusual or abnormal examples, it seems to me seriously wrong as an account of normal cases. When I am attending in the way suggested to one part of my visual field, the rest of it is not somehow blank or indeterminate. It still has a perfectly specific and determinate character, and one which is still there in or before consciousness, even though not attended to. If this were not so, it would not be part of my *visual* field at all, since the very idea of a visual field is that of a visual expanse or array of which one is conscious. One way of defending this point is to notice that when I shift my attention to another part of the field, I have no sense that the part I am now attending to has just "popped" into existence; phenomenologically it is not at all like directing a searchlight in a new direction and having something emerge out of previous darkness.

Second. Connected with this is Pollock's suggestion [53] that being aware of the content of one's sensory experience can only be understood as having a belief about it. This seems to me even more clearly mistaken. If I am asked about the character of a certain part of my visual field, I can attend to that part and thereby arrive at a belief about its contents. In doing so, it is about as clear from a phenomenological standpoint as anything could be that I have an independent and logically prior awareness or consciousness of the relevant part of the field, upon which the belief is based and in relation to which it may be judged as accurate or inaccurate in varying degrees. And as long as beliefs are understood as conceptually formed, propositional states, it is equally clear that in any normal state of sensory awareness there is much of which I am aware that is captured only imperfectly or incompletely by any such belief, something that may be underscored by my continuing attempts to refine and improve the conceptual description so as to make it more adequate to that of which I am independently aware.

Third. Thus while it is perfectly correct that in an ordinary perceptual frame of mind, a person has beliefs about physical objects and not about the content of sensory experience as such, this in no way shows that he or she does not also have a correlative consciousness or awareness of the nonconceptual content of that experience that guides the formation of the physical-object beliefs on the basis of the tacitly grasped correlation that I speak of in my paper. The perceiver does not normally focus on or attend to this nonconceptual experience, but it still constitutes the only evidence he or she has for the correctness of the resulting beliefs about the physical world, thus raising the issue of whether and why it is good evidence. This is the issue I am concerned with at the end of my paper, and which I hope to have a good deal more to say about eventually. It is an issue that critical epistemology cannot, I believe, avoid, and upon which Pollock's alternative epistemological approach sheds no light at all. Thus while I have no quarrel at all with his pursuit of his epistemological project, he has said nothing that convinces me that it is not at least equally important to pursue mine.

To Plantinga

I will confine my reply to Plantinga to what I see as the three main issues that divide us. In some of what he says about these issues, Plantinga seems perhaps not to have fully understood my argument, but I do not think that our differences result entirely or even mainly from such misunderstanding.

First. Plantinga claims that the awareness of the sensuous content of an experience cannot, in the way that I claim, be a reason for a basic belief about that content

> because it is simply not the right sort of animal to serve as a reason: it is not itself a belief; it does not itself have a truth-value; it is not itself something from which something can be inferred; it does not itself possess propositional content. [63-64]

This is of course essentially the same point that was made by Davidson in the passage that was quoted and discussed in my paper, a point to which I thought that I had made an effective reply (one that Plantinga does not really discuss). Nevertheless, I will try again.

Suppose that I am aware of a large patch of red in the middle of my visual field. I am of course forced here to give a conceptual description of the patch and my experience of it in order to indicate the sort of experience I have in mind, but the experience itself is of course nonconceptual or sensuous in character. Suppose that I also come at the same time to have the propositional and conceptual belief that there is a patch of red in the middle of my visual field. I might arrive at such a belief as an attempt to conceptually describe the patch of which I am nonconceptually aware or it might be suggested in some other way, e.g., by a question posed by someone else. Now for me to be even capable of having such a belief, I have to understand that its content ascribes to me, albeit approximately and imperfectly, just the sort of nonconceptual experience that, as it happens, I am actually having: to have just that sort of nonconceptual experience is what it is to have a large patch of red in the middle of my visual field. Since I am aware of the nonconceptual content of the experience and understand the descriptive, conceptual content of the belief, I am in an ideal position to see that the two are in accord, thus having, I claim, an outstandingly good, essentially conclusive (though not quite infallible) reason for thinking that the belief is true. To be sure, the nonconceptual awareness that furnishes this reason is, as Plantinga points out, not a belief, not something that has a truth-value or that has propositional content. But this merely shows, I suggest, that the initially plausible principle that all reasons must take such a form turns out to be mistaken.

Where exactly Plantinga would disagree with the foregoing account I am unable to tell from his remarks. It might be suggested, I suppose, that the issue is merely verbal: whether the sort of basis for belief that I have in this case deserves to be called a *reason*. The term seems to me entirely appropriate, since my awareness of nonconceptual content is something of which I am conscious that enables me to tell or judge that my belief is correct. But nothing much hangs on the term, and one could say instead, as I just did, that I have a basis rather than a reason for thinking that the belief is true.

In fact, I doubt very much that Plantinga's objection is merely a verbal point of this sort. But having been able to glean from his comments no further idea of just what that objection might be, I will have to let the matter rest here for now.

Second. Plantinga also expresses uncertainty about the conception of justification that I am employing. His suggestion, based on my use of the idea of being in an ideal position to tell whether a belief about my experience accords with the nonconceptual content, is that on my view justification, or at least noninferential justification, has in general to do with being in a good or ideal position or condition to judge whether the belief in question is accurate. This leads him in turn to ask why looking at a chair in good light at close range does not constitute being in a sufficiently good position for the belief to be justified.

All this is, however, largely misconceived, since the suggested view of justification is not the one that I hold. In my view, for a belief to be justified in the epistemic sense is simply for the believer to have a good reason for thinking that it is true, where *having* such a reason requires that one have direct conscious access to it. (Indeed, I would be on the whole quite happy to abandon the term "justification" to externalists and their ilk, and to simply couch the issues with which I am concerned in terms of such reasons.)

Thus the issue with regard to beliefs concerning physical objects such as Plantinga's chair is whether we have such reasons for them; and if so, what form those reasons take. Since I have no conscious access to the chair that is direct in the relevant sense (a point to be further considered momentarily), the perceptual belief that there is a chair present cannot be basic or foundational in the way described in my paper, which is, I claim, the only way in which a contingent, empirical belief can be basic or foundational. Thus some other sort of reason needs to be found if beliefs of this sort are to be justified in the sense I am concerned with.

It would be possible to attempt an account of such a reason along the lines suggested by the account of justification that Plantinga mistakenly attributes to me. One could appeal to the fact that I am in a position that is excellent for forming such beliefs, together of course with the fact that I have indeed spontaneously or noninferentially formed that particular belief. Indeed, I attempted an account along these lines in *The Structure of Empirical Knowledge* (1985). The problem, however, is that at least the first of these premises itself requires some sort of justification.[4] Since the coherentist account attempted in that book clearly does not work,[5] and since externalist and contextualist views are in my judgment also unacceptable, the justification of this premise will have to appeal sooner or later to foundationally justified beliefs—so that this view fails to constitute a genuine alternative to foundationalism.

Thus, I suggest, the only apparent place to look for a good reason for a perceptual belief of the sort in question is to the specific character of the nonconceptual experience involved in the perceptual state. It is, after all, because that experience has one such character rather than another that there appears to me to be a chair present rather than a table or a tree or an airplane. No doubt it is true, as Plantinga and Pollock both suggest, [61, 53] that from an intuitive standpoint the experience "presents" the chair to me, which is, I think, just to say that I normally take utterly for granted a correlation between the various features of nonconceptual experience and various kinds of physical objects and situations, forming beliefs accordingly, with nothing even approximating deliberate consideration or inference. But merely the fact that this correlation between experience and the physical world is accepted and relied on without question or reflection in no way constitutes a justification for it or for the resulting beliefs. And thus if such beliefs are to be justified or even in principle justifiable, some further account needs to be given of the nature of this correlation and of why beliefs formed in accord with it are likely to be true. As far as I can see, such an account can only appeal to the details of the experiential features and to their relations with each other.[6]

Third. Plantinga also asks why I am not, in Fumerton's terms, directly acquainted with the chair when I perceive it directly before me. Though I have suggested that my account of foundational beliefs may be a more perspicuous way of putting the sort of insight that acquaintance theorists were getting at, I prefer not to couch my own view in these terms and so will leave to Fumerton the job of directly answering Plantinga's query. I am quite sure, however, that Plantinga means to also be asking why such a belief cannot be foundationally justified according to my account, and it is this question to which I want to briefly respond.

The simple answer is that on my view, it is only the sort of constitutive or "built-in" awareness that one has of the contents of one's own conscious states that can justify foundational beliefs, since only this sort of awareness raises no further issue of justification. The chair itself is not something that I am aware of in this way, since it is not itself part of the content of a conscious state.

This is not, of course, to deny that I have conscious states that depict or represent the chair and thus in a certain sense bring it "before my consciousness." But while I can and do have foundational beliefs about the representational content of such states, the claim that these representations are *correct* obviously depends on more than that content and thus transcends the scope of foundational justification. This is obvious in the case of a belief, where having a built-in awareness of its content does not suffice for its justification; but it is equally true of the nonconceptual sensory content, whose status as constituting an appearance of a certain sort of physical object and thus as "presenting" that object to the mind depends on precisely the correlation between sensory features and physical situations already discussed, a correlation for which some further justification is urgently needed.

Notes

1. Pollock seems to recognize [46] that there are different epistemological projects, but his account here does not seem to me to adequately recognize the specific and very traditional project with which my paper is concerned.

2. I have some nervousness about Pollock's use of this term, which may embody some theoretical baggage of its own, and I will generally avoid it, recasting matters in terms of sensory experience.

3. It could be and in fact has been questioned whether we have any way of deciding whether a reason is genuinely cogent, as opposed to whether it is cogent according to our accepted standards, but a reply to this essentially skeptical line of thought is beyond the scope of the present discussion.

4. The second premise does too, unless it is claimed to be basic or foundational; but it will be simpler here to focus on the first premise, which clearly does not have foundational status.

5. See the paper cited in note 1 of my main paper in the present volume.

6. For an initial stab at such an account, see (BonJour, forthcoming, b), which partially overlaps and further develops the ideas of the paper in the present volume.

Reference List

Armstrong, D. (1963). "Is Introspective Knowledge Incorrigible?" *Philosophical Review* 72: 417-32.

Ayer, A. J. (1956). *The Problem of Knowledge*. London: Cambridge University Press.

Bergmann, G. (1964). *Logic and Reality*. Madison: University of Wisconsin Press.

Berkeley, G. (1965). *The Principles of Human Knowledge*. C. M. Turbayne (ed.). *Berkeley: Principles, Dialogues, and Philosophical Correspondence*. Indianapolis: Bobbs-Merrill.

BonJour, L. (1985). *The Structure of Empirical Knowledge*. Cambridge: Harvard University Press.

———. (1991). "Is Thought a Symbolic Process?" *Synthese* 89: 331-52.

———. (1997). *In Defense of Pure Reason*. London: Cambridge University Press.

———. (forthcoming, a). "The Dialectic of Foundationalism and Coherentism." J. Greco and E. Sosa (eds.). *Blackwell Handbook of Epistemology*. Oxford: Basil Blackwell.

———. (forthcoming, b). "Foundationalism and the External World." J. Tomberlin (ed.). *Philosophical Perspectives*. Atascadero, CA: Ridgeview Publishing Co.

Cheng, P. W., and K. J. Holyoak. (1985). "Pragmatic Reasoning Schemas." *Cognitive Psychology* 17: 391–406.

Chisholm, R. M. (1989).*Theory of Knowledge* (3d ed.). Englewood Cliffs, NJ: Prentice Hall.

Chomsky, N. (1957). *Syntactic Structures*. The Hague: Mouton and Company.

Davidson, D. (1983). "A Coherence Theory of Truth and Knowledge." D. Henrich (ed.). *Kant oder Hegel*. Stuttgart: Klett-Cotta.

Firth, R. (1959). "Chisholm and the Ethics of Belief." *Philosophical Review* 68: 493-506.

Fumerton, R. (1976). "Inferential Justification and Empiricism." *The Journal of*

Philosophy 73: 557-69.

——. (1985). *Metaphysical and Epistemological Problems of Perception.*
Lincoln, NE: University of Nebraska Press.

——. (1990). *Reason and Morality: A Defense of the Egocentric Perspective.*
Ithaca, NY: Cornell University Press.

——. (1995). *Metaepistemology and Skepticism.* Lanham, MD: Rowman &
Littlefield.

Goldman, A. (1979). "What Is Justified Belief?" G. Pappas (ed.). *Justification
and Knowledge.* Dordrecht: Reidel.

Goodman, N. (1955). *Fact, Fiction, and Forecast.* Cambridge, MA: Harvard
University Press.

Haack, S. (1993). *Evidence and Inquiry: Towards Reconstruction in
Epistemology.* Oxford: Basil Blackwell.

Jackson, F. (1997). *Perception.* Cambridge: Cambridge University Press.

Lehrer, K. (1974). *Knowledge.* Oxford: Clarendon Press.

——.(1990). *Theory of Knowledge.* Boulder: Westview Press.

Lewis, C. I. (1943). *An Analysis of Knowledge and Valuation.* La Salle, IL:
Open Court.

Locke, J. (1975). *An Essay concerning Human Understanding.* P. H. Nidditch
(ed.). Oxford: Oxford University Press.

Mackie, J. L. (1976). *Problems from Locke.* Oxford: Oxford University Press.

Moser, P. (1989). *Knowledge and Evidence.* London: Cambridge University
Press.

Nozick, R. (1981). *Philosophical Explanations.* Cambridge, MA: Harvard
University Press.

Plantinga, A. (1988). "Positive Epistemic Status and Proper Function." J.
Toberlin (ed.). *Philosphical Perspectives 2: Epistemology.* Atascadero, CA:
Ridgeview Publishing Co.

——. (1992). "Justification in the Twentieth Century." E. Villanueva (ed.).
Philosophical Issues 2: Rationality in Epistemology. Atascadero, CA:
Ridgeview Publishing Co.

——. (1993a). *Warrant: The Current Debate.* Oxford: Oxford University
Press.

——. (1993b). *Warrant and Proper Function.* Oxford: Oxford University
Press.

——. (2000). *Warranted Christian Belief.* New York: Oxford University Press.

Pollock, J. (1974). *Knowledge and Justification.* Princeton: Princeton University
Press.

——. (1987). *Contemporary Theories of Knowledge.* Totowa, NJ: Rowman &
Littlefield.

——. (1995). *Cognitive Carpentry.* Cambridge, MA: MIT Press.

Pollock, J., and Cruz, J. (1999). *Contemporary Theories of Knowledge* (2d ed.). Lanham, MD: Rowman & Littlefield.

Popper, K. (1959). *The Logic of Scientific Discovery*. New York: Harper.

Price, H. H. (1950). *Perception* (2d ed.). London: Methuen.

Quinton, A. (1973). *The Nature of Things*. London: Routledge & Kegan Paul.

Rorty, R. (1979). *Philosophy and the Mirror of Nature*. Princeton: Princeton University Press.

Rosenthal, D. (1986). *Philosophical Studies* 94: 329-59.

———. (1991). "Two Concepts of Consciousness." D. Rosenthal (ed.). *The Nature of Mind*. New York: Oxford University Press.

Russell, B. (1912). *The Problems of Philosophy*. Oxford: Oxford University Press.

———. (1984). *Theory of Knowledge: The 1913 Manuscript*. E. Eames (ed). London: Allen & Unwin Ltd.

Sellars, W. (1963). "Empiricism and the Philosophy of Mind." *Science Perception and Reality*. London: Routledge & Kegan Paul.

———. (1975). "The Structure of Knowledge." H. Castaneda (ed.). *Action, Knowledge, and Reality: Critical Studies in Honor of Wilfrid Sellars*. Indianapolis: Bobbs-Merrill.

———. (1981). "The Lever of Archimedes." *Monist* 64: 3-36.

Strawson, P. F. (1979). "Perception and Its Objects." G. F. MacDonald (ed.). *Perception and Identity*. Ithaca, NY: Cornell University Press.

Wason, P. (1966). "Reasoning." B. Foss (ed.). *New Horizons in Psychology*. Harmondsworth, England: Penguin.

Index

access, 21, 44, 49, 52. *See also* internalism, strong access
acquaintance, 13, 14, 23, 31, 44, 49-51, 52, 53, 55, 60-65, 72-73; with external objects, 16, 31, 50, 61-65, 74-76, 84; with mathematical and logical facts, 61, 73-74; theories, 4, 70
antifoundationalist dilemma. *See* Sellarsian dilemma
antirealism, 17
Armstrong, D., 10
awareness, 44; immediate, *See* acquaintance; of objects, 53-55; of sensory content, 29, 52-55, 59, 72, 80, 81, 82

beliefs: basic or foundational, vii, 21, 22-23, 51-52, 64-65, 83, 84; incorrigible, 42-43, 62; infallible, 9-12; nonfoundational, viii; prima facie justified, 42; second-order or meta, *See* justification; self-evident, 23; self-justifying, 23; too few appearance beliefs for foundations, 43-44, 71-72, 80
Berkeley, G., 36

Chisholm, R. M., 31, 35-36

Chomsky, N., 47
cognition, 44-45; innate, 48; procedural knowledge of, 45-48
coherentism, 22, 83. *See also* skepticism
common sense methodology, ix, 46-48
competence/performance distinction, 47
concepts, always relational, 16-17
consciousness, 26-28
contextualism, 22, 83. *See also* skepticism
correspondence, 14-15
critical epistemology, 79-80

Davidson, D., 29
Descartes, R., viii
direct acquaintance. *See* acquaintance
direct apprehension, 23, 52
direct realism, 42
doxastic: assumption, 41, 44-45, 48; theories, 41-42. *See also* foundationalism, doxastic

entailment, 19-20n7
epistemic norms, 48, 69
epistemological projects, alternative, xii, 69, 79-80

About the Contributors

Laurence BonJour is professor of philosophy at the University of Washington. He is best known for his work in epistemology explicating and defending the coherence theory of justification. In addition to numerous articles, he has authored *The Structure of Empirical Knowledge* (1985) and *In Defense of Pure Reason* (1997).

Richard Fumerton is professor of philosophy at the University of Iowa. He works in epistemology, metaphysics and value theory. He has published many articles as well as three books: *Metaphysical and Epistemological Problems of Perception* (1985), *Reason and Morality: A Defense of the Egocentric Perspective* (1990) and *Metaepistemology and Skepticism* (1995).

Alvin Plantinga is the John A. O'Brien Professor of Philosophy and the director of the Center for Philosophy of Religion at the University of Notre Dame. His research interests include epistemology, metaphysics and the philosophy of religion. His three most recent books focus on epistemology: *Warrant: The Current Debate* (1993), *Warrant and Proper Function* (1993) and *Warranted Christian Belief* (2000).

John L. Pollock is at the University of Arizona, where he is professor of philosophy and research professor of cognitive science. His work in epistemology and artificial intelligence on defeasible reasoning is particularly well known. He has authored ten books, including two editions of *Contemporary Theories of Knowledge* (1999 and 1987), *Cognitive Carpentry* (1995) and *Knowledge and Justification* (1974).